D1647950

LUTHER
the
Preacher

LUTHER
the
Preacher

FRED W. MEUSER

AUGSBURG Publishing House • Minneapolis

LUTHER THE PREACHER

Library of Congress Catalog Card No. 83-72107
International Standard Book No. 0-8066-2051-X

Manufactured in the United States of America

Contents

Dedicated to
All who preach
All who are awed by the privilege
And all who want to preach better

Foreword

This book, *Luther the Preacher,* emerges from Dr. Fred W. Meuser's Hein lectures of 1983.

The C. C. Hein Memorial lectureship is an annual series of three or four lectures instituted by the American Lutheran Church in memory of Dr. C. C. Hein (1868-1937), the first president of the former American Lutheran Church.

The lectures are currently under the administration of the Division for Theological Education and Ministry of the American Lutheran Church and a steering committee which includes the president of the church, the presidents of Luther Northwestern, Trinity, and Wartburg Seminaries, and the director of the Division for Theological Education and Ministry.

Scholars of Lutheran and other Christian churches are invited to present the Hein lectures in alternate years. The lectures are presented in four seminary communities: Trinity Lutheran Seminary, Columbus, Ohio; Wartburg Theological Seminary, Dubuque, Iowa; Luther Northwestern Theological Seminary, St. Paul, Minnesota; and Pacific Lutheran Theological Seminary, Berkeley, California.

This 1983 production, highlighting the 500th anniversary of Luther's birth, marks the 41st year for this distinguished lecture series.

WALTER R. WIETZKE, DIRECTOR
DIVISION FOR THEOLOGICAL EDUCATION AND MINISTRY
THE AMERICAN LUTHERAN CHURCH

Preface

I love good preaching. I hear it often in seminary and every week in my home parish. But good preaching doesn't just happen. It is a learned skill that deserves more attention than it gets in many seminaries and pastors' studies.

I also love Luther. In 15 years of teaching church history my interests became so wide-ranging that I never became an expert on one particular area. The longer I taught, the more I was attracted to the ancient church on the one hand, and the modern church on the other. But my interest in Luther never waned. He was a fantastic human being! For the Hein Lectures, in the 500th anniversary year of his birth, I could choose no other topic. Even the subject of a new Lutheran church didn't stand a chance. It just had to be Luther.

But which aspect of Luther? Why not the one most frequently ignored by scholars and writers? Look through all the publicity of all the programs and publications of this anniversary year. If you can point out one, even one, that features a single lecture or program on Luther the preacher, you will be my guest for dinner at a restaurant of your choice. Literature on Luther the preacher is virtually non-existent in English. Professor Harold Grimm's short book of the 1930s, *Martin Luther as a Preacher*, makes a bit of a start. The best treatment I have found in English is the 14-page section on Luther's preaching in James MacKinnon's *Luther and the Reformation*, vol. 4. A few Ph.D theses of modest quality are available on microfilm. In no language is there a definitive book on Luther the preacher. Yet that is the single most intimate point of contact between Luther and many of us preachers and hearers. The topic seemed a natural.

Luther's Passion for Preaching

When the preacher speaks, God speaks

The story of Staupitz's conversation with Luther in the garden in 1511 is a familiar one: "You are to become a teacher of Scripture and preacher to the monks in the monastery." Luther protested, because his own inner spiritual struggles had not yet been resolved. Staupitz was adamant. Luther finally said, "It will kill me, I won't last three months." Staupitz replied by saying, "God has many problems and is in need of wise people in heaven, too." [1]

We have no way of knowing whether Luther then sensed what he saw later about the immense responsibility of preaching. Perhaps he was just thinking of how difficult it is to preach to others when one is in the agony of the struggle for personal faith. Imagine how much more plaintive his protest would have been had Staupitz said to him what in later years he frequently said to others about the office of preaching: "When the preacher speaks, God speaks!"

Even now I am startled and frightened by this. It conjures up memories of sermons—my own and those of others—that I would never want to blame on God! Who would

11

dare equate the word of a sinner-preacher, always deficient in insight and partly blind to God's revelation, with the very word of God? Luther would, and he often did. He stated that when a preacher steps down from the pulpit, he may say defiantly "with St. Paul and all apostles and prophets . . . 'Here God speaks.' God himself has said it. And I repeat it . . . whoever cannot boast like that about his sermon should leave preaching alone, for he surely denies and blasphemes God." [2]

In a sermon on the Easter Gospel, he said that like the angel who announced the resurrection, preachers must be sent from heaven. "So the pastor must be sure that God speaks through his mouth. Otherwise it is time for him to be quiet." [3] "Yes, I hear the sermon; but who is speaking? The minister? No, indeed! You do not hear the minister. True the voice is his; but my God is speaking the word which he preaches or speaks." [4]

For Luther, preaching was not a preacher's ideas stimulated by the prod of a text. It was not human reflections about God and life. It was not searching around in one's personal religious insights for some kind of contemporary message that one thinks people need. Christian preaching— when it is faithful to the word of God in the Scriptures about our need and God's response to it — is God speaking. When it focuses on what God has done for the world in Jesus Christ, it is God speaking. When it invites faith and presents Christ so that faith becomes possible, it is God speaking. It is God's very own audible address to all who hear it, just as surely as if Christ himself had spoken it.

So clear and insistent was Luther on this that Heiko Oberman has said, "The Reformation had its own *ex opere operato* doctrine, not in connection with the sacraments, the visible Word [as in Catholicism], but with the audible word. The sermon . . . [is] the certain presence of the Word of God in the mouth of the preacher." Oberman points out that this is not only Luther's and Lutheranism's

12

view of preaching, but also, through Henry Bullinger and his *Confessio Helvetica Posterior,* the "common doctrine for the whole Reformation . . . the equation of the preached Word with the Word of God." [5]

Much is made of the doctrine of the real presence in Luther's sacramental theology. He also had another "real presence" — the real presence of Christ in proclamation. When the proclamation about Christ is the biblical message of God's judgment and grace, not only is the preacher's word God's word, but when the preacher speaks, God is really present and speaking. In the sermon one actually encounters God. That makes preaching — and hearing — a most dangerous business.

For Roman Catholicism, preaching was either instruction about God whom one really meets and receives in the sacraments, especially the Mass, or it was instruction in the law of Christ, which showed how to live once one had received God through the holy sacrament. But pre-Reformation Catholicism had no sense of a drawing near or actual self-giving of God (the real presence of Christ) through preaching. That was Luther's contribution. God is present in the word. If we are touched by the word, God has touched us. If we grasp and trust the word of promise, we have communion with God. We need not go beyond the word to God. The word is not just preliminary to the sacraments, a kind of lower stage of God's presence that we really get in the sacraments or, as many would say today, in prayer or special kinds of spiritual experiences. The word brings God with all God's gifts.

To repeat, in the preaching of the word of God, the living God is actually present to seek us out and move into our hearts. According to Emanuel Hirsch,

> This is the most characteristic and the most profound thing which Luther said about preaching. No Christian preacher since Paul, so far as I can see, ventured to follow out this

thought to the full. If anywhere, then here, the circle between the Reformation and the time of the apostles is complete. The boldness with which Paul speaks of his preaching office in 2 Corinthians 3 and 4 comes to life again in Luther.[6]

Luther set the preaching of the apostles and our preaching precisely on the same level. We simply continue until the last day what they began. Our preaching is just as much a fulfillment of the Markan command to preach as was that of the apostles. No longer is there any real difference between our preaching and that of the apostles, as if God were more present then or their preaching had a different kind of authority. If the gospel is the same, then it is the same word of God. The same God also speaks with the same power in *our* preaching.

According to Luther, this is the real apostolic succession. In contrast to Osiander, some 19th-century Bavarian Lutherans, and some Swedish theologians, Luther did not connect apostolic succession to a succession of ordained preachers. For Luther, every proclamation of the gospel, wherever and by whomever, is truly preaching, in that it is the word in which God comes to us and requires faith. Even the head of a household has an office of preaching. Wherever God gives someone living perception to bear witness in truth, there God is truly present. That presence is neither tied to the clergy, nor in any way to the person of the preacher, nor to any continuum of the laying on of hands in ordination. It is tied to the message. When the message is God's, then, "when the preacher speaks, God speaks."

Luther went so far as to say that our preaching and Christ's preaching are the word of God in the same sense, and that the very preaching of Christ continues in our preaching. In a way, ours even exceeds Christ's, because God has graciously given to our words (that is, to those

14

who came after Christ) an effect in numbers and out-
reach that even Christ's words did not have in his day.[7]

Such confidence is not easy to come by. It did not come
easily to Luther, and it was not easy for him to retain it—
as we shall see at the end of this chapter. But inherent in
such confidence is the trust that God is saying,

> Just go on preaching. Don't worry about who will listen;
> let me worry about that. The world will be against you,
> don't let that trouble you. Nevertheless others will be there
> who will listen to you and follow. You do not know them
> now, but I know them already. You preach and let me
> manage.[8]

Luther said he himself preached as a wanderer sings in the
woods: the trees hear and the echo answers. That was
enough. "Whom it hits, it hits." [9] That's the way it goes.
And that's God's business.

In his last sermon in 1546, Luther said,

> In times past we would have run to the ends of the world
> if we had known of a place where we could have heard
> God speak. But now that we hear [God speak] every day
> in sermons . . . we do not see this happening. You hear at
> home in your house, father and mother and children sing
> and speak of it, the preacher speaks of it in the parish
> church—you ought to lift up your hands and rejoice that
> we have been given the honor of having God speak to us
> through his Word.
>
> Oh, people say, what is that? After all, there is preaching
> every day, often many times every day, so that we soon
> grow weary of it. . . . All right, go ahead, dear brother, if
> you don't want God to speak to you . . . at home in your
> house and in your parish church, then be wise and look
> for something else: in Trier is our Lord God's coat, in
> Aachen are Joseph's pants and our blessed Lady's che-
> mise; go there and squander your money, buy indulgence
> and the pope's secondhand junk. . . .

Aren't we stupid and crazy, yes, blinded and possessed by the devil? There sits the decoy duck in Rome with his bag of tricks, luring to himself the whole world with its money and goods, and all the while anybody can go to baptism, the sacrament, and the pulpit! How highly honored and richly blessed we are who know that God speaks with us and feeds us with his Word. . . . But these barbarous, godless people say: What, Baptism, sacrament, God's Word? —Joseph's pants, that's what does it! [10]

In spite of his sarcasm, Luther's deepest conviction was that the Holy Spirit will fill the hearts of some hearers through faithful preaching. These will know that when you speak the word of God, God is truly speaking. And as a preacher, that's the spirit in which one should approach the task.

Nothing except Christ is to be preached

Won't preachers who think their words are God's words become arrogant and domineering? Won't they forget that "God's thoughts are higher than our thoughts and God's ways than our ways"? Aren't there already too many preachers who think too highly of their own preaching? Why accentuate a problem that is bound to exist in every sinful proclaimer: to think more highly of oneself than one ought to think?

Luther's answer to this was: *Nihil nisi Christus praedicantur*—"Nothing except Christ is preached," by which he meant, "Nothing except Christ is to be preached"—Christ as Savior, God's great gift, the one in whom God shows his own face, in whom God has spoken a clear, definitive, once-for-all word to the world. When Christ is preached as good news, as the prophets and apostles present him, then "when the preacher speaks, God speaks," and the Holy Spirit produces faith, hope, love, and a joyful new life. Preaching Christ Jesus as Lord means knowing oneself as a servant of the word and its hearers, for Jesus' sake. Such preachers of Christ not only know their subservient place in the scheme of things, but are content with it.

Whoever, therefore, does not know or preach the gospel is not only no priest or bishop, but he is a kind of pest to the church, who under the false title of priest or bishop, or dressed in sheep's clothing, actually does violence to the gospel and plays the wolf in the church. [11]

A Palm Sunday 1521 sermon on Matt. 21:1ff begins, ". . . a preacher in the Christian churches should be judged by this — that he preaches Christ alone, so that the people may know in what they may trust and on what to base their conscience." [12] In his Easter sermon a week later he said,

The priests have no other office than to preach the clear sun, Christ. Therefore, preaching is a dangerous thing. Let the preachers take care that they preach thus or let them be silent. A bad preacher is more dangerous than a thousand Turks. . . . Whoever does not preach about God's kingdom has not been sent by Christ. . . . Now to preach God's kingdom is nothing else than to preach the gospel which teaches faith in Christ — through which alone God dwells in us.[13]

Of particular importance in the context of our contemporary Holy Spirit movement are his words, "The Holy Spirit wants to preach only Jesus Christ; the poor Holy Spirit doesn't know anything else." [14] "Where the devil does not find Christ he has already won the game." [15]

Christ is to be preached, only Christ, Christ in the details of his earthly life and not merely in doctrinal form. Through Christ as he lived with people in daily life we see who he was and is for us. Through the Christ of the Gospels God is made known and in that life God stands at our side and comes to our aid. Luther loved the Gospels, immersed himself in the Gospels, lived and relived the

17

events of Christ's life in the Gospels, and above all sub-
merged himself in the words of Christ in the Gospels.
Without Christ's words, his deeds would mean nothing.
Luther said we are to dwell on Christ's words, for they
will bring us life.

Luther's critics have often accused him of being so pre-
judiced in favor of Paul that he almost ignored the rest of
the New Testament. His doctrinal preference for Romans is
well-known. Not nearly so well-known is the fact that of all
the sermons he preached—probably over 4000 [16]—and of
the 2300 that have been preserved, only about 30 were on
Romans. That is less than 1½%. Ten of those were on the
first part of Romans 12 ("living sacrifice. . . . Do not be
conformed . . . but transformed. . . . not to think more
highly than he ought to think. . . . one body . . . many
members. . . . gifts that differ"). [17] It is often implied that
he pushed the Gospels aside in favor of a few favorite
Epistle texts which became the touchstone for everything
else in Scripture. Those who have read his sermons know
better. Sheer numbers don't prove anything, but he has
more than 1000 sermons on the synoptic gospels alone, plus
many hundreds on John.

Emanuel Hirsch says,

> In truth he pulled the Gospels out from under the bench
> just as much as he did Paul. He . . . bound the whole life
> of faith into them. It is no accident that in [the church
> which bears his name] as in no other, the humanity of the
> Lord has become the center point of all theological work,
> and that his church has sung about the Lord and his death
> in a fashion unheard of before that time.[18]

In every trait of the human Christ of the Gospels, God
is revealed. Every act and especially every word which reveals the meaning of what Christ did has inside of it
all the characteristics of God that are theologically expressed in the doctrine of justification. Justification perme-

ated Luther's theology, but the living, breathing, loving, serving, and suffering Christ permeated his preaching. Compare the random sermons on Romans with the many hundreds of sermons on John's gospel, his favorite. His series on John 16–20 lasted almost a full year in 1528–29. In 1531–32 he spent almost a year and a half on John 6–8. He preached more on John's gospel in a year than on Romans all the rest of his life! To be sure, the gospel-preaching was always permeated by the spirit of Romans — but his point of departure and the focus of his preaching was the human Jesus of the Gospels.

By "preaching Christ" he did not, however, mean the constant repetition of his name that characterizes some "Jesus-preaching" today. Luther knew well the medieval kind of Jesus-preaching that dwelt emotionally on his sufferings and whose purpose was no deeper than to rouse pity for the suffering Jesus; or the *"imitatio Christi"* preaching that exhorted the hearers to so-called acts of discipleship. Luther's great hymn of repentance and faith, *"Aus tiefer not schrei ich zu dir"* ("Out of the Depths I Cry to You," *LBW* 295) is a powerful, personal proclamation of the gospel even though it never mentions the name of Christ. So it can be with preaching. Luther was sensitive enough to know that an overly heavy stress on the name of Christ may be a conscious or subconscious way to cover up shallow preparation. He was not one who had to say "Jesus" every two minutes on schedule in order to assure himself that he was preaching Christ.

As you would expect, preaching Christ meant, above all, preaching his passion and resurrection. Some day someone ought to try to do with these sermons what Roland Bainton did with Luther's Christmas preaching in *The Martin Luther Christmas Book*.[19] I have no idea how many specific sermons he preached on passion texts (the extant ones surely run into many hundreds), but the theme—the human Jesus Christ, one of us, bearing our sin and its guilt, alienating power, and corrupting effects to the cross and into death for us—breathes in every sermon. So also does the resurrection (see Chap. 3).

In Luther's preaching, Christ is our brother, substitute sin-bearer, atoner, deliverer, liberator, and victor. All the biblical themes are there — the bearer of our sin and guilt and the one who on our behalf conquers God's enemies: evil, sin, and death. All the classic theories of the atonement appear side by side in his preaching, with no sense of disparity, contradiction, or need for rational harmonization. He did not, like Gustav Aulén in his *Christus Victor,* Anselm in *Cur Deus Homo?,* or most theologians of the atonement, pick out one theme as dominant or superior. He let each one (including what we call the "Abelardian" theory, that the essence of atonement is the breaking down of our barriers to God by Christ's act of total loving self-sacrifice) do its own work and bestow its own gift. If a theme was in the Scripture and was a sign of God's grace in action for us, he proclaimed it. That may be one of the advantages preachers have over systematicians.

One of the captivating and frustrating things about Luther is that everything he knew about Christ had a way of creeping into every text. If you took his Christmas sermons literally, you could easily conclude that when the Son of God emerged from Mary's womb the whole of redemption was completed. When Christ permitted himself to be baptized by John, his identification with all sinners was so complete that one might think he could have ridden the wings of the dove back to heaven without any shortchanging of his redemptive career. So with the temptation in the wilderness, the feeding of the 5000, the healing of the paralytic, and most especially the Lord's agony in Gethsemane. Here, he said, is the pinnacle of the passion, the actual, profound, personal, spiritual, inner battle behind his death. Here he faced all the forces of terror and despair for us and conquered them. Luther didn't regard the rest as a picnic, but in some ways Gethsemane was the climax. Of course, he said similar things about his trial, the bearing of the cross, and especially the experience of being forsaken, which wrung "My God, my God" from Christ's lips.

From this side of the resurrection, wherever Luther saw redemption he saw *all* of redemption. And if exegetically he found more in a text than was really there, at least he did not preach Christ in little disconnected bits and pieces, expecting the hearers to be able to assemble them into a whole. He would much rather have had too much of Christ in a given sermon than too little. It may not solve all of our interpretive and exegetical questions, but we surely get a clue concerning Luther's "Preach nothing except Christ," to hear him say, "If in a text I find a nut with a shell too hard to crack, I fling it on the Rock [Christ] and I get the sweetest kernel [out of it]." [20]

In Luther's context, "preaching nothing except Christ" also meant something highly practical and contemporary—clarifying the place, function, and character of good works. Luther was hung up on them. Couldn't he think of anything else to say? Were they really so big a problem that no matter what the text, he had to go off on a tangent on the value or lack of value of our efforts and actions in the sight of God? Whether he was preaching on the Wise Men at Epiphany, the Magnificat, the stilling of the storm, "Peace I give to you" on his way to Worms, who is to receive the sacrament, or the last sermon of his life (at Eisleben in 1546) on "I thank thee, Father . . . that thou hast hidden these things from the wise and understanding and revealed them to babes" — whatever the text, he made God's way of salvation crystal clear: not by our efforts, but by God's gift.

Not only indulgences, pilgrimages, alms, repetitious prayers, and other so-called churchly good works felt Luther's lash repeatedly, but also every innate human drive to be worthy of something good from God, to get God into a spot where he somehow owes us something. Luther knew not only the Scriptures; he also knew people. And from the way in which, year after year, he glorified God's goodness, undeserved grace, and promises despite our unworthiness, we can conclude that it was as hard for the Wittenbergers to say yes to God's judgment on their lives and no to the innate urge to bargain with God as it is for us today. The persuasiveness and clarity of his words makes one wonder why he needed to say it so often, but he also gives us a bit of comfort in our need to speak again and again to the particular perversions of the gospel in our day. Today's barriers may be more subtle, and that constitutes one of the major tasks for our preaching homework.

Most of us are familiar with the theological debate over law and gospel in Lutheran theology. Are they always to be distinguished and kept separate? Are they enemies of one another? Is the key mark of a Lutheran preacher to be able rightly to distinguish law and gospel, as both Luther and C.F.W. Walther have said? Is its function only to condemn? Must the law always be preached prior to the gospel? Or is the law itself part of the gospel, itself an expression of God's saving will, God's "You belong to me" assurance, as Ronald M. Hals says in his essay, "Luther and the First Commandment"? [21] Does the law bring only awareness of sin and judgment, while the gospel brings only assurance?

However we approach and answer these questions, a reading of Luther's sermons quickly shows that his basic concern was rather simple. He was not primarily interested in a theoretical definition of law and gospel. Rather, he was concerned to show that nothing we do can bridge the gap, restore us to God, and give us new life. God's grace and forgiveness make us alive. Nothing else does. So long as we are still in a tug-of-war or a bargaining stance with God, we are dead. Only God's promise makes us alive, and our trust in God's promise makes all questions about the worth of our efforts superfluous.[22]

In his preaching, Luther's concern over law and gospel was not the theological definition of their relationship, but a very pastoral one, namely, Where is your trust? What do you count on and lean on for assurance and well-being? Where is the focus of your life — on your own efforts, or on God's promises in Christ? Is the grace of God the focus of your Christian life, or is it instead the question, How am I doing spiritually?

One other touchstone in Luther as to whether Christ alone is really being preached is, Are people whose conscience is distressed finding assurance? Comfort and assurance were high priorities for him, not only for the bereaved, but for those who were burdened, tempted, or, like Luther, crushed by their own unworthiness. Although in the pulpit he spoke very little and with great reserve about his own continuing battle with doubt and despair (his *Anfechtungen*), his empathy for others who had the same experience shaped what he saw and centered on in the text. Just as he tended to find the whole Christ and all his saving work in every text, so he opened up the assuring message of text after text.

Notice how gently the Savior deals with wounded spirits, he said to the Wittenbergers, how friendly he is to publicans and sinners, how patiently he bears with the disciples who misunderstand him, what compassion he had for lepers, for the woman whose son had died, for the centurion and his servant, for blind Bartimaeus, the woman at the well, and the woman taken in adultery. When preaching to people who, like Luther himself, had been taught to think of both God and Jesus as threatening, demanding, critical, and distant (and taught to run to Mary and the saints as compassionate intercessors), Luther delighted in speaking of the Lord as friend of sinners, one who made them feel at home and at ease in his presence. Once he

23

discovered the compassionate Christ, his Lord's powerful pull on him never waned.

Luther seldom spoke in mystical terms, and in spite of his down-to-earth language about God, never in buddy-buddy or cozy terms about Christ. Yet it is not inaccurate to say that Luther deeply loved Jesus — the beautiful, caring, human Jesus of the Gospels. Any sermon that failed somehow to hold up that Lord — whose love reached its pinnacle in his self-giving on the cross — so that others could be amazed, as he had been, and then be drawn to trust in the promises and find peace with God and with self, could not be described as preaching Christ.

In his later years, as he saw people applying the assurance of the gospel to themselves when they had no business doing so, this emphasis faded somewhat. Preaching to disturb the conscience then became more frequent, but never an end in itself. It always remained a means — for many, a necessary step — toward the assurance that is God's will and gift for all. Unless the comfort and assurance of the gospel flooded the congregation, Luther felt that Christ had not been preached.

Toward the end of his life he became so disgusted with the Wittenberg community that he wrote to Katie to sell the Wittenberg property and move to the farm: "I would rather live as a vagabond and a begger than to live out my poor old last days in martyrdom and turmoil with that disorderly crowd." [23] Yet even then he never ducked the "gospel-centered" texts in favor of the "law-centered" ones: [24]

In an Ascension Day sermon of 1534 Luther said,

> If you preach faith [and assurance] people become lax. . . . But if you do not preach faith, hearts become frightened and dejected. . . . Do as you please. Nothing seems to help. Yet faith in Christ should be preached, no matter what happens. I would much rather hear people say of me that I preach too sweetly . . . than not preach faith in

Christ at all for then there would be no help for timid, frightened consciences. . . . Therefore I should like to have the message of faith in Christ not forgotten but generally known. It is so sweet a message, full of sheer joy, comfort, mercy, and grace. I must confess that I myself have as yet not fully grasped it. We shall have to let it happen that some . . . turn the message into an occasion for security and presumption; others . . . slander us . . . and say [that by preaching so much of Christ] we make people lazy and thus keep them from reaching perfection. Christ himself had to hear that he was a friend of publicans and sinners. . . . We shall not fare any better.[25]

Preaching as an eschatological conflict

If the reality of God speaking through the preacher and the call to preach Christ alone were not enough to make preaching a wondrous, dangerous, and passionate affair, Luther found another aspect worth noting. Often he said that a sermon is comprised of teaching and exhortation (*Lehre* and *Ermahnung*). "So St. Paul divides the office . . . ." Teaching lays out for the people what is true; exhortation encourages them to believe it and live it. "Both parts are necessary for the preacher, which is why St. Paul also practiced both." [26] It all sounds calm and intellectual: inform the mind and exhort the will. Ulrich Neubach is insistent that Luther understood preaching as precisely that: instruction and exhortation.[27]

But that's not the way Luther preached. He preached as if the sermon were not a classroom, but instead a battleground! Every sermon was a battle for the souls of the people. Heiko Oberman says that for Luther, a sermon was an apocalyptic event that set the doors of heaven and hell in motion, a part of the actual continuing conflict between the Lord and Satan. It is the most dangerous task in the world because "where Christ appears, there the devil starts to speak." [28] The sermon — and the congregation that hears it — is a battlefield "in the eschatological struggle between Christ and the adversary." The sermon's aim is to "make Christians of the hearers through the Word of God and thus hurl the power and victory of Christ against the power of evil." [29]

For Luther, "the Word and its proclamation are the weapons by which God subdues His enemies and frees [people] from bondage." [30] Vajta sees every sermon as part of the cosmic warfare that began with the incarnation and "continues after Christ's death and resurrection in spite of the victory which he obtained. The Word, written and preached, is the sword with which he pursues his struggle up to the last day." [31] Through the spoken word the power and victory of Christ invade life today. Preaching is therefore not only about the saving acts of God. The sermon is itself a saving event. [32] Aside from this war, the word and what it sets in motion in the souls of people cannot be understood.

When God speaks, things can never be the same again. God's word arrests the hearer, touches, condemns, offers, draws, and appeals. No one can listen in cool detachment or stay out on the perimeter in a neutral stance. We cannot go out in the same relationship to God as when we came in. If we remain neutral, we have turned our backs on God; the devil has won at least that skirmish. When the word about Christ is preached, God has spoken and one answers yes or no. There is no other alternative.

God speaks! Christ alone is to be proclaimed! The sermon is a battleground on which God and Satan contend for the hearts of the people! How will we approach the task of preaching if we really believe this? How much study, care, effort, and prayer will we want to put into it? It is no wonder that Luther called preaching the highest calling of all.

Whoever has received the call to . . . preach has the highest office in Christendom imposed on him. Afterward

26

he may also baptize, celebrate mass, and exercise pastoral care. If he does not wish to do so he may confine himself to preaching and leave baptizing and lower offices to others as Christ and the apostles also did.[33]

Luther — weary of preaching

How did all this work out in Luther's own life as a preacher? If a preacher can carry on through thick and thin in the confidence that it is God's business to worry about the results, then surely Luther never had the problems of discouragement, disillusionment (today we say "burnout"), of wanting to quit. Wrong. Not only did this father of Reformation preaching, this clearest herald of the gospel since the time of Paul *want* to quit, he *did* quit — for a time — in disgust and hopelessness.

Luther was not the pastor of the Wittenberg congregation. Johannes Bugenhagen (or Pomeranius, as he is often referred to) held that position from 1521 until 1558, twelve years after Luther had died. Yet Luther, also, preached to that congregation regularly, usually several times a Sunday as well as during the week. Normally one would preach at two services Sunday morning, again in the afternoon, and at services every weekday. It is a miracle that two or three preachers could manage it. Luther preached because the congregation asked him to, and because his doctorate in theology was understood by him and his contemporaries to be a call to teach the word of God to the whole church. That included preaching. Never a weekend off — he knew all about that. Never even a weekday off. Never any respite at all from preaching, teaching, private study, production, writing, counseling.

Review his life in the 1520s for a moment: (1) It began with Worms, the great public confession and defiance. (2) Then came the ban of the empire — open season on Martin Luther, except where he was protected by his prince. (3)

Because of his insistence that the gospel be proclaimed freely, he was active on many fronts: theological, ecclesiastical, political, social, personal, and familial. (4) His job as professor of Bible at the university was full-time work of its own. (5) He wrote theological treatises by the score: biblical, homiletical, liturgical, educational, devotional, and political, some of which have shaped Protestant church life for centuries. (6) All the while he was translating the whole of the Scriptures into German, a language that he helped to shape by that very translation. (7) He carried on a voluminous correspondence, for he was constantly asked for advice and counsel. (8) Travel, meetings, conferences, and colloquies were the order of the day. (9) All the while he was preaching regularly to a congregation that he must have understandably regarded as a showcase of the Reformation (and which his foes watched with hawkeyes for opportunities to discredit what he was doing).

In the midst of all that activity, in 1528 he preached almost 200 times! From 1529 we have 121 sermons, even though severe headaches and spells of dizziness were becoming frequent. On 40 days that year he preached twice. His was a remarkable and tireless preaching ministry. His productivity was prodigious, almost miraculous.

Suddenly, however, at the beginning of 1530, he quit. From January until early April he stayed out of the Wittenberg pulpit (except on Jan. 23 and 30, when he preached as a special favor to the prince, and one sermon on March 20).[34] From April 15 until September he did a bit of preaching on his way to and while at Castle Coburg during the time of the Augsburg Colloquy. He could not attend, because he had no legal protection there. The Wittenberg congregation did not hear him again until the fall of 1530.

In February, Melanchthon wrote to Mykonius of his hope that Luther would not give up preaching for good. George Rörer, another close friend who took notes on every sermon he heard Luther preach, wrote in March that "we are all dismayed that Dr. Martinus doesn't intend to preach publicly any more." [35] Yet how often Luther had said, as in a sermon on Exod. 7:3-5 in 1524, that the reason we preach is because

. . . . we are bidden [by God] to preach . . . we are not bidden to justify people and make them pious. This . . . should comfort all preachers . . [the] word he is to proclaim even though no one may want to listen to him. . . . If I could be moved by the fact that my word and sermon are despised, I suppose I would not go on preaching. But [says God] go on, Moses, preach! If you are despised because of it, commit that to me.[36]

What happened? It's simple. He just became totally discouraged, in spite of what he had advised others. In 1529 he had warned the congregation several times that he would stop preaching unless there were more fruit of the gospel among them. He told them they were selfish and miserly. "I am sorry I ever freed you from the tyrants and papists. You ungrateful beasts, you are not worthy of the Gospel. If you don't improve, I will stop preaching rather than cast pearls before swine." [37] Read his "Happy New Year" to them in 1530. The text is the circumcision of Jesus. He started out calmly enough:

For us he put himself under the law, to free us from the power of sin, so we may live in obedience to the gospel. Christ alone is the fulfiller of the law. All of your comfort, life, righteousness and joy are in Christ. . . . Believe that firmly. Then at once good works will follow — thanksgiving and praise of God and service of the neighbor with all one's property and goods. Those who do not give to a brother are not pious. In times past people gave for temples and altars, now everybody scrapes everything together for himself. There is nothing [going on] but scraping and scratching! But in two years the Turk will be at your door. Just don't think you are safe. If you were pious you would accept the word, trust God, do good to the neighbor and take heed to your calling.[38]

That is exactly what he said they were *not* doing. He warned the "shameless self-avengers who fill the streets at night with weapons and swords" that if they "don't willingly keep the peace [they] will be forced to keep it! . . . Watch out that you do not fall into God's vengeance."[39] He compared the congregation to Capernaum in Jesus' time and lamented over them in language like that in Jeremiah 20:[40]

> The time will come when you who now have an abundance of preaching . . . will long for a single sermon. But your impudence is so great that you have no appreciation for preaching. . . . I am unwilling to preach [to you] any more. . . . I would rather preach to raving dogs because there's no use doing it with you and it is offensive to me. So— I shall leave preaching to the pastor and his assistants. I will stick to my lecturing.[41]

In letters, he mentioned their ingratitude, lack of any self-discipline, firing of guns under his window, hardheadedness, shameless dress, adultery, profiteering, and thievery. And the ones who didn't do those things just laughed at the ones who did! Worst of all was their drunkenness, which he called the great vice of "us Germans." There was even "swilling and yelling in the taverns at the very time of the worship services." Wittenberg was full of the gospel, but only a minority received it. If they didn't want to hear God, they would have to hear the devil. Instead of the glorious joy of being freed from God's wrath, the people sought the freedom of the flesh. They were proud of the gospel, but there was nothing behind it.[42]

Some interpreters see psychological or pathological illness in all of this. Obviously, Luther was angry. But above all he was disillusioned. I think that preachers, especially, can understand Luther's state of mind. At the start of a new year or a new decade, it is natural to review the year past, compare one's very high hopes at the beginning with the harvest one sees, and think of what lies ahead. "If these people are so religiously insensitive, I would do better to invest my energies elsewhere. I've had it 'up to here.' I'm too tired to take it any more. Let someone else do it." Luther knew that state of mind. He was ready to quit, and from New Year's until he left for Castle Coburg in April, he hardly preached in Wittenberg.

Read what he said on Aug. 27, 1531, after he had been back in the pulpit for almost a year. The pain and discouragement still show through, even though the call to preach had once again revived. The sermon was on 2 Cor. 3:4-6: "Such is the confidence that we have through Christ toward God. . . . our competence is from God, who has made us competent to be ministers of a new covenant. . . ."

The office of preaching is an arduous office. . . . If I could come down with a good conscience, I would rather be stretched upon a wheel or carry stones than preach one sermon. For anyone who is in this office will always be plagued; and therefore I have often said that the damned devil and not a good man should be a preacher. But we're stuck with it now. . . . If I had known I would not have let myself be drawn into it with twenty-four horses. Ingratitude is our reward. . . . And for this we have to let the peasants and noblemen starve us until we feel like turning in our key and saying, "Go, preach yourselves, in the name of all the devils!" . . .

The townsmen, the fellows who, when they have read one book are full of the Holy Spirit, are the worst. If I were to follow my own impulse I would say, "Let the damned devil be your preacher!" So I have often thought, but I cannot bring myself to do it. But then our confidence returns and we say, let it happen what may, we still have our confidence through Christ. . . .

I cannot boast of anything higher except that I am preach-

31

ing by God's command and will; it is his will and I know that it is not fruitless. . . . [even when] our own people are chewing up the gospel. But we must shut our eyes and look to Him and remember that I did not invent this Word of God and this office. It is God's Word, God's work. . . . It didn't grow in my garden. . . . It is our confidence . . . that God has qualified us to be ministers, and . . . also that we shall not preach in vain. . . .

It's a rotten office to have to deal with these people . . . to suffer such physical misery and give an accounting on the last day, that a man would rather be a swineherd. But this is our consolation. . . . if it pleases God, good enough . . . . I wouldn't risk a hair of my head to uphold my office. But if it pleases God, I'd like to see the fellow who would knock it down. . . . If somebody else can do better . . . I would help to pay him myself. . . . I know what preaching is. . . . God is my Lord, the world is my enemy. The fruit will come [that is our confidence]. [But to] wish to stop their mouths and persuade people not to despise me or to be grateful, this confidence we must not have. [43]

Read the first sermon Luther preached at the Coburg after leaving Wittenberg and compare it with the passage just quoted. It is a sermon on the cross and suffering. There is not a single reference to Wittenberg or to his withdrawal from the pulpit. But if you know what lies behind it, you will be fed and strengthened in your own struggle with discouragement. It is a classic sermonic presentation of the theology of the cross: what suffering for Christ's sake is all about. Suffering "that we may be conformed to him" is the kind "we have not chosen ourselves." "When it comes we are to patiently bear and suffer it. . . . Christ, for His Word's sake, will not only help us bear [it] but also turn and transform it to our advantage." Christians' suffering comes "because we hold to the Word of God, preach it, hear it, learn it, and practice it." Therefore the promises of God to "do something remarkable with our suffering" are the tree we can hold onto when we are about to be swept away. If you have affliction and suffering, be comforted by the fact that you have not chosen it yourself. Then "let him take care of it or fight it out."

> If you give yourself to Scripture, you will feel comfort and all your concerns will be better. . . . When we stay with the Word and hold on to it, we shall certainly have the experience of conquering and coming out of it fine. . . . our Lord God . . . puts us in a tight place, so that we may learn from our own experience that the small, weak, miserable Word is stronger than the devil and the gates of hell. . . . Since it is better to have a cross than to be without one, nobody should dread or be afraid of it. [44]

To the clergy assembled at Augsburg in 1530, he wrote:

> No message would be more pleasing to my ears than the one deposing me from the office of preaching. I suppose I am so tired of it because of the great ingratitude of the people, but much more because of the intolerable hardships which the devil and the world mete out to me. But the poor souls will not let me rest. Then, too, there is a man whose name is Jesus Christ. He says no. Him I justly follow as one who has deserved more of me.[45]

Of Luther's return to the pulpit in Wittenberg Matthesius simply said,

> Luther refrained from preaching until his zeal, that is, the holy wrath cooled — or rather until it [reignited] his own calling in his heart so that he again mounted the pulpit.[46]

When in the fall of 1530, following his return from the Coburg, he again began to preach, it was almost as if nothing had happened. Consistent with his general practice of *not* making his own spiritual struggles prominent in the pulpit, he did not showcase the depth of his struggle. Never again to the end of his life did he take a leave from preaching, except for illness or travel. In 1531 he was back to 180 sermons — one every two days. When on the road, he was always pressed into the pulpit by hosts and friends.

Not that he wasn't tempted to quit on other occasions, but the Scriptures, he said, overcame the temptation because "they constantly testify to the God who still has not gotten tired of loving the fallen world and calling it back to himself." [47] If he is tireless in his love, he shares that tirelessness with us or restores it when our disillusionment has driven it away. Luther remained a preacher of the gospel, not because he had been too pessimistic about Wittenberg or the world, but because God loved the people still, because only the word of both judgment and grace could help them, and because only God is to determine when the proclamation of the gospel is to cease. That this might happen in Germany someday, Luther always felt to be an awful possibility. But until God renders that judgment, the call to his preachers to preach stands firm, and all God's promises of strength, courage, and help remain in force.

This crisis of 1530 did, however, leave a permanent mark on Luther. After 1530 he was different. No longer did he expect the whole world to be won to the gospel. Believers would always be a minority. His expectations became more realistic, his spirit more cautious and chastened. Yet even in his very last sermon, just three days before he died (which he ended by saying, "Much more could be said about this Gospel but I am too weak"), even then the passion for preaching — as voice of God, herald of Christ, and soldier of the Spirit — still flamed. Those of us who have been called by God as fellow preachers of the same gospel could do worse than to let that passion inspire and shape our preaching.

Luther's Style
of Preaching

Problems in recovering Luther's preaching

If you should pick up one of the 22 volumes of Luther's sermons in the Weimar edition of his works, you could be in for a surprise. They're not in German! The sermons of this father of the modern German language, who is said to have preached in the language of the people like none before him, are a duke's mixture of German and Latin, often more Latin than German. Of course, Luther wrote most of his treatises in Latin, for that was the language of theologians. But why the sermons? Did he really run the two languages together in such a way that today it takes an expert linguist to make it through a single paragraph? Did the common people really know Latin so well that they could understand such a mishmash of two languages?

The answer to both questions is no. Luther did indeed preach in German. He almost never used a Latin word from the pulpit, and he never used preaching to show off his amazing knowledge of Greek and Hebrew. The reason for the confusion is that even though he preached in German, he never wrote out his sermons. (Sometimes he did expand them into major essays after having preached them.) He usually took into the pulpit with him what he called his *Konzept:* a brief outline or plan — written in German — of how he would proceed. Friends who were university-trained (sometimes also monastically trained) took notes while he preached. They often spoke and wrote Latin at least as well as they did the vernacular. Latin was concise and accurate, almost a shorthand by comparison with German. When Luther preached, German went into the ear of these note-takers, and without any strenuous mental effort, a mixture of Latin and German flowed out through their pens.

Imagine trying to recover the genuine Luther of the pulpit from those mixed German-Latin notes! First of all, such note-takers weren't always present. Second, when there were several of them, their notes often differed significantly from one another (editing occurred in the very hearing and writing). Third, later editors, studying these various records, compared, assembled, and edited them into a single transcript.[1] Fourth, someone had to retranslate the Latin back into the German that Luther might have used.

How much of Luther's actual style would endure such a process? Preachers know how little their style shows through a simple mimeographed sermon transcript. When I pick up a manuscript of that "great sermon" I preached just a few years ago, my reaction often is, "Where did it go? What happened to it? It was a lot better than that when I preached it." Imagine what it might look like after having survived the above process — and after 450 years had elapsed!

Furthermore, when you read Luther's "sermons," for example the ones in vol. 52 of the American edition of *Luther's Works,* you may be reading sermons not intended for the pulpit and sermons that were never preached. Only a few volumes of the 55 in *Luther's Works* contain preached sermons. Some of what are published as sermons really weren't. They are the so-called *postils*. This word has come to mean simply "exposition." A standard form for starting an exposition of Scripture in Luther's time was to say, "according to these words of sacred Scripture," which in Latin is *"post illa verba sacrae scripturae." Post illa,* which means only "according to these," became the popular designation of such textual expositions. Postils are sermon-like treatments of the pericopes written by Luther in order to help the new evangelical preachers.

Luther did not divide these 16th-century sermon helps into exegetical and homiletical sections, but wove them together in a much more sermonic form, usually far longer and more detailed than any sermon could be. For example, in vol. 52 of *Luther's Works,* which includes his postils on the Gospels for seven services between Christmas Eve and Epiphany, the so-called sermons vary in length from eleven pages on Luke 2:15-20 (for the early service on Christmas morning) to 127 pages on the Matthean account of the Wise Men for Epiphany Sunday.

When we remember that Luther wrote these sermon helps during his months of hiding at the Wartburg Castle with no library available, one gets some idea of his broad knowledge of Scripture in the original languages and his amazing grasp of history and literature. With very few books at his disposal he produced the epochal translation of the New Testament into German and also the Advent, Christmas, and Epiphany postils.

Frequency of preaching and breadth of background

Luther and his contemporaries surely should have known how to preach—they did enough of it. A quick review of the weekly Wittenberg congregational calendar would show no organizations such as our parishes have. The activity was worship: services on Sunday at 5:00 A.M. with a sermon on the Epistle, again at 10:00 with a sermon on the Gospel, and again in the afternoon on one of the lessons, the Old Testament, or the Catechism; Mondays and Tuesdays sermons were on the Catechism, Wednesdays on Matthew's gospel, Thursday and Friday, the Apostolic Letters were used; Saturday late afternoon was usually devoted to John's gospel.

Over the years Luther also wove in long sermon series on whole books of the Old and New Testaments. These services — and especially the preaching — were to do the whole job (except for instructing children) that our more complicated programs of education, study, and fellowship are supposed to do. In addition, the Sunday afternoon devotions in Luther's home were no rushed three-minute affair read out of 16th-century equivalents to *Portals of Prayer* or *Christ in Our Home*. Often they lasted an hour or more, with Luther, as head of the household, again preaching a sermon to family and guests (of which there were usually many). When he could manage it, Luther did a special series on the Catechism four times a year, each series lasting two weeks, with four sermons per week. That alone added 32 more sermons a year. Most years he preached over 100 times. Among the slower years were 1522, with 46 sermons, and 1540, with 43.

To be honest, one would have to say that almost everything Luther did was preaching. We divide his works into categories such as academic, theological, sermonic, devotional, pastoral, catechetical, and polemic—and there are significant differences between them in approach, intent, content, and style. But these differences are not nearly as sharp as we might assume. His lectures were never technical or objective, no matter how precise his treatment of a word or how incisive his analysis of a theological issue. Always he aimed at the heart as well as the mind of a student. He felt he had not dealt responsibly with any text, in classroom or pulpit, if the hearer's understanding and personal appropriation had not been deepened and strengthened.

Last year in a seminar I led on Luther we read a variety of his treatises, doctrinal writings, commentaries on Galatians, lectures on Genesis and John, expositions of Psalms, devotional and pastoral writing, correspondence, and sermons. Both the students and I were surprised how hard it was at times, unless one remembered the title of the work, to know just which category any particular one fit into. They were all proclamation, and they all spoke to the heart as well as the head. So when we talk about Luther's preparation for preaching, we must include the whole broad range of all his study—not just the final step of getting ready for the next Sunday morning.

The priority of preaching and qualities of the preacher

Since I ended the first chapter with the interlude of Luther's deep discouragement, it is worth noting that this period was an exception to his general spirit about preaching. During those very difficult years, in fact, just after he started preaching again, he said, "If I could today become king or emperor, I would not give up my office as preacher." [2] At a time when we sometimes talk about church officials, bishops, and seminary professors as having moved up the ladder, it is interesting to note Luther's comment that since all pastors are under the obligation to preach, there are no real ranks among them:

There is only one obligation, that of preaching. And the gradations have to do with the frequency with which this duty is fulfilled. A pastor who preaches is more than a bishop who dedicates bells and churches, confirms children and sprinkles holy water. These externals have no meaning to God. [3]

Countless times, in referring to the preaching task, he called it a unique, heavily burdened, and dangerous calling that stands under the sobering caution of the Lord himself. Preachers will have to give account to God for every idle word they speak. Who could be so presumptuous as to grasp this calling for oneself? Only in obedience to the very call of God would one dare to accept it and carry it out. But "there is that man Jesus." [4] When he calls, we may respond in confidence that he will equip and sustain us.

Luther's Works, especially the Table Talk, abound with hints to preachers and portrayals of the good preacher. One such passage has ten points: 1) Be able to teach so people can follow you; 2) Have a good sense of humor; 3) Be able to speak well; 4) Have a good voice; 5) Have a good memory; 6) Know when to stop; 7) Be sure of one's doctrine; 8) Be ready to venture body and blood, wealth and honor, for the word of God; 9) Suffer oneself to be mocked and jeered at by all; 10) Be ready to accept patiently the fact that nothing is seen more quickly in preachers than their faults.[5] It sounds like the kind of list Luther probably spun off the top of his head. Of course, somebody wrote it down and it quickly became canonized as Luther's Ten Commandments for preachers, whether he was that serious about it or not. Another list has three others heading his Decalog: Stand up, speak up, shut up.[6] There were times when he violated the third of these commandments.

Sermon preparation

Luther was not very oblique when he wrote in the introduction to John Spangenberg's *Postil* in 1542,

Some pastors and preachers are lazy and no good. They do not pray; they do not study; they do not read; they do not search the Scripture . . . as if there were no need to read the Bible for this purpose. . . . They are nothing but parrots and jackdaws. . . . The call is: watch, study, attend to reading. In truth you cannot read too much in Scripture; and what you read you cannot read too carefully, and what you read carefully you cannot understand too well, and what you understand well you cannot teach too well, and what you teach well you cannot live too well . . . the devil . . . the world . . . [and] our flesh are raging and raving against us. Therefore dear sirs and brothers, pastors and preachers, pray, read, study, be diligent . . . this evil, shameful time is not the season for being lazy, for sleeping and snoring.[7]

Study, yes—Scripture above all. Preaching always meant opening up, proclaiming, setting loose the word of God in the Scriptures by speaking it heart to heart. In the speaking, in the living word, the *viva vox evangelii,* not primarily the word read as lessons or the word read privately, the Holy Spirit leads people to Christ, touches their hearts, works repentance and faith, bestows the gifts of the Spirit. Without the word spoken by a believer, the gospel cannot do its work. The proclaimed word is the effective form of the word. "Where the oral proclamation of the Gospel ceases the people will revert to heathenism in a year's time. . . . The devil cares nothing about the written Word, but where one speaks and preaches it, there he takes to flight."[8] The command to the apostles was to preach, not to write—and Luther even tweaked their noses a bit for having written without an express command of Christ. They did it, he said (with considerable knowledge of history), only because the truth about Christ was in danger of being perverted or of slipping away.

For Luther, the indispensable speaking of the word in preaching was always exposition of Scripture. Not only was his conscience captive to the written Word of God, so was his preaching.

> This is the sum of the matter: Let everything be done so that the Word may have free course instead of the prattling and rattling that has been the rule. . . . We can spare everything except the Word. . . . We profit by nothing as much as by the Word. Everything else must pass away no matter how much care and trouble Martha invests in it. . . . God help us to achieve this. Amen.[9]

In this reference to the Word he meant Scripture. Christ was the Word supremely, to be sure. The message about him is the word. Not everything in Scripture is of equal import. He knew that. But our access to it is always through the witness of apostles and prophets in the Scripture. And to speak it, one must know it and its central purpose clearly. He probably did not mean this as a test for ministerial candidates, but he once said, "He who has only one word of the Word of God and is not able to preach a whole sermon on the basis of this one word is not worthy even to preach." [10] He referred to the Scriptures as a great tree which poured down beautiful, fresh, tasty fruit every time he shook its branches.

By "shaking the branches" of Scripture Luther meant study. Correct understanding is a gift of God that we receive not through brooding over the Word until the light goes on, but through serious study of the text.[11] Personal faith and contemplation are necessary, of course, but never as a substitute for painstaking study, including philological research. Neither can take the place of the other. The best way to go to the Bible is in the original languages. One should use commentaries (including the postils) only if necessary:

> It is better to see with one's own eyes than with another's. On this account. . . . I would wish that all my books were burned. Otherwise everybody will just imitate me.[12]

> One cannot preach the word of God if one does not master the languages. History [yes] illumines God's work and

God's word, [but] the languages are the scabbards in which the sword of the Spirit is sheathed.[13]

It is a sin and shame not to know our own book or to understand the speech and words of our God; it is a still greater sin and loss that we do not study languages, especially in these days when God is offering and giving us men and books and every facility and inducement to this study, and desires his Bible to be an open book. O how happy the dear fathers would have been if they had our opportunity to study the languages and come thus prepared to the Holy Scriptures! What great toil and effort it cost them to gather up a few crumbs, while we with half the labor — yes, almost without any labor at all — can acquire the whole loaf! O how their effort puts our indolence to shame! [14]

The Scriptures are the vessel, the casket, the larder in which the gospel—the sword of the Spirit, the jewel, the wine, the food—are stored. Scripture is not obscure if one knows the languages.

. . . although faith and the gospel may indeed be proclaimed by simple preachers without a knowledge of languages, such preaching is flat and tame; people finally become weary and bored with it, and it falls to the ground. But where the preacher is versed in the languages, there is a freshness and vigor in his preaching, Scripture is treated in its entirety, and faith finds itself constantly renewed by a continual variety of words and illustrations.[15]

How great it would be if that were an iron-clad guarantee! Educated preachers who have mastered all the skills and the languages were needed, said Luther, "at least in our time since we must speak to many . . . different kinds of people other than just neighbor Hans." [16]

Of the letters of the princes it has been said that they should be read three times. But the letters of God (for so

St. Gregory calls Scripture) are to be read three times, seven times, yes seventy times seven times, or . . . an infinite number of times. Because they are divine wisdom which cannot be so easily comprehended at first glance. If . . . anyone reads Scripture casually, as well-known and easy material, he is deceiving himself . . . by no means imagine that you know it. In the morning read a psalm or other Scripture and study it for a while. That is what I do. When I get up in the morning I recite the Ten Commandments, the Creed, and the Lord's Prayer with the children, adding any one of the Psalms. I do this only . . . to keep myself well-acquainted with these matters and I do not want to let the mildew of the notion grow that I know them well enough. The devil is a greater rascal than you think. You do not as yet know what sort of fellow he is and what a desperate rogue you are. His definite design is to get you tired of the word and . . . draw you away from it. This is his aim.[17]

Why such hard work? Fear of misleading the flock, if nothing else, ought to be enough to drive the preacher to this kind of study. "The preacher must die daily through concern that he may lead his flock astray." [18]

The greatest evil on earth is a false preacher. He is the worst man on earth. No thief, murderer or scoundrel on earth can be compared to him. They are not as wicked as a preacher who dominates people in God's name . . . and leads them into the abyss of hell through [his] false preaching.[19]

Preparing sermons is hard mental and spiritual work, little appreciated by people who don't do it. He said,

Sure, it would be hard for me to sit "in the saddle." But then again I would like to see the horseman who could sit still for a whole day and gaze at a book without worrying or dreaming or thinking about anything else. Ask a *Cantzelschreiber,* a preacher or speaker, how much work it is to speak and preach. . . . The pen is very light, that is true. . . . But in this work the best part of the human body (the head), the noblest member (the tongue), and the highest work (speech) bear the brunt of the load and work the hardest, while in other kinds of work either the hand, the foot, the back or other members do the work alone so the person can sing happily or make jokes freely, which a sermon writer cannot do. Three fingers do it all [the work of writing] . . . but the whole body and soul have to work at it.[20]

Seldom, however, in his preparation did Luther write out a full manuscript of a sermon, except for the postils, perhaps because he was so busy writing all sorts of other works for publication. In fact, with his prodigious output of manuscripts for publication, one wonders how he ever made time to prepare for preaching. And to that he never gives us a clue! He kept no time chart, no diary from which we might reconstruct some "typical" days. Of his *Konzepts* (outlines), only a few have ever been found. He seems not to have kept a sermon file—amazing since he was called upon to preach at every drop of the hat.

How much of a brother Luther is to those of us who struggle and agitate over our preaching can be seen in his admission that he occasionally dreamed of entering the pulpit without being prepared to speak.[21] Whether during those tough nights he shared the fairly common preachers' dream of entering chancel or pulpit without pants on, we have no way of knowing.

Luther's preaching method

Almost everyone has heard that Luther marked a watershed in the history of preaching. Up until his time the heart of the Christian life was seen in the sacraments, which gave the power of God's grace to enable Christians to do good works. In recognition of these, God then gave

45

more grace. In the Reformation the heart of Christian life and of the sacraments was seen to be in the word of promise, the message about the amazing love of God in Christ. Through that message, God's favor, grace, and gifts are bestowed freely. Faith, trust, love, joy, and obedience are the result. So the purpose of preaching was radically changed. Through the proclamation God comes to us as Christ is proclaimed. Of course, a sermon is a Christian schoolroom, granary, and battleground, but above all it is an encounter with God, through which God intends to bestow the fullness of his gifts. The sermon definitely is not optional in Christian worship, and it is not a way of filling time before the real star of the show—the sacrament—makes its appearance.

All of this meant a change in the form of the sermon. Before Luther's time there was preaching in abundance.[22] But most sermons were rather highly structured addresses that developed some subject chosen by the preacher: a theological question, a particular virtue or sin, a problem of the Christian life. There was a rather set pattern. First was the introduction, then the question was divided into many parts and analyzed. Preachers marshaled philosophical arguments to prove their case, citing the Fathers as authorities, with points and subpoints, main teachings and subteachings, logical precision and speculative ability. Depending on the preacher, there might be more or less Scripture in a sermon. Often the saints were very prominent. However, the sermon was not taken with utter seriousness, because the sacrament was all-important.

With Luther, especially after 1521, came what many interpreters call a totally new form of the sermon: *die schrift-auslegende Predigt. Schriftauslegend* is usually translated as "expository." *Auslegen* literally means "to lay out," to exhibit or display, to make something evident or plain. Luther had long since come to the conviction that such a laying out of the plain central message of Scripture was priority number one in the needed correction of the church's teaching and life. From the start of his preaching ministry he gave much greater place to Scripture than almost any of his contemporaries. After 1521 this switch was complete and permanent. Listeners are to hear God speaking in his saving power and presence in sermons. The aim of the sermon is therefore to help hearers understand the *text*, not just a religious truth. Its goal is that God may speak a gracious word through a text so that the people may be given faith or be strengthened in faith by the Holy Spirit. Its method is to take a given segment of Scripture, find the key thought within it, and make that unmistakably clear. The text is to control the sermon. When the sermon is over, the people are to remember the text and its primary message much more than the sermon. The sermon is to follow the flow of the text, the language and the dynamic of the text, and not impose its own direction or dynamic from without.[23]

Luther's method has often been called that of the *homily*, but that is really inaccurate. A homily usually moves verse by verse, without tying the whole together. Luther insisted on finding the *Sinnmitte*, the heart of the text. That heart, that *Kern* or kernel is to save the preacher from getting lost in details. Every story has a *Herzpunkt* which the preacher must find and return to again and again. Every time he preached on the entry into Jerusalem Luther landed feet first on "Behold your king comes to you!" even though no one sermon was just like any other.

The main point of a sermon is to be so clear in the preacher's mind that it controls everything that is said. If that is clear, then the rest of the sermon may be allowed to flow with considerable freedom. "In my sermons I bury myself to take just one passage and there I stay so the hearers may be able to say 'That was the sermon.'"[24] And that's the way he did it. We have Luther's sermons on the Sunday Gospels over many years. No two are the same in structure or development. Yet every time that he preached on the desire of the people to make Jesus their king, he stood face-to-face with the firm will of Jesus to lead the people past "sign-faith" to trust in the "naked word."

Luther rejected the art of fancy introductions in favor of a simple statement of the text's center: "In this Gospel our Lord tells us that God is merciful to those who suffer." Or, "Here God tells us that He hides Himself from the wise and reveals Himself to the simple." Or (preaching on Christ's baptism), "Is this not a beautiful glorious blessed exchange in which Christ changes places with us, takes our sin upon Himself and gives us His innocence and purity?" On special occasions such as weddings, baptisms, and funerals, there was more of an introduction, but ordinarily he started with, "What does the text want to tell us?" Then he went right into it!

Many of us were taught to preach on a well-formulated, short, and preferably striking theme which would be developed—perhaps by analysis of the text, perhaps according to a superimposed scheme—in two or three fairly symmetrical parts. My homiletics professor even timed every class sermon to see whether the parts consumed fairly equal amounts of time. That system has served me well over the years, and I still show the effects (and, I hope at least occasionally, the blessings) of it in my preaching. Such a system was totally foreign to Luther. It might even have alarmed him, because it probably would not sound textual enough, and it allows too much room for preachers to import their own "thing" into sermons or to make sermons artful or even artificial.

Luther could not have been less interested in symmetry, external form, beauty of expression, alliterative phrases, plays on words, balance, polish, or other signs of the rhetorical art. He had seen too much of that in the preaching against which he rebelled not to be deeply suspicious of it. He would have regarded books of snappy sermon starters or canned illustrations as the presence of the very devil. Everything calculated or artful tends to push the heart of the text and the natural flow of the word of God into the background. All such homiletical tricks and playing with words (as he would call it), such toying around with proclamation are unfitting to the task. He also suspected that they masked an unworthy desire on a preacher's part to be popular.

Such a desire for popularity was seen as the preacher's death trap.

> There is no greater evil or poison than vainglory. . . . she is the bride of the devil . . . [and] works great harm in a preacher. It moves him to say . . . [I] must preach . . . so that the people may say: "This preacher will turn out to be a fine man. He [can] . . . produce something different and new." Then people gape and say: "He is certainly a fine preacher; he knows how to hit the nail on the head; I have never heard anyone put it this way." And so the man is puffed up with pride, tickled with the praise, and imagines that he is an ox when he really is scarcely a toad. Then he must be very careful not to spoil things with the people. Because they praise him, he must, in turn, praise them. So they praise one another until one goes to the devil with the other.[25]

Luther would not like the style of the preaching of my two pastors (although he would love the content) because they work hard on the sermon's form, theme, and parts. They always preach on a carefully chosen theme so that you can follow the logical progression from one major part to another. They come up with interesting and often humorous introductions (not thigh-slappers, but chucklers), and they both love plays on words, which they use unusually well in service of the gospel.

Luther's only device, if it could be called that, was to set things in opposition to each other. He loved to employ tensions: *law/gospel;* conflict: *sin/grace, God/Satan;* paradox: *free will/bound will;* and above all, dialog, at which he was a master. Dialog is part of a very high proportion of his sermons. Usually he spoke in the first person for both parties. There is conversation between Luther and his hearers, between God and humanity, God and Adam, Jesus and the disciples, God and Satan, Luther and Satan, sin and righteousness, life and death, and heaven and hell. In almost every sermon two sides confront each other. This is as close as Luther came to a designed form, but he did it so naturally that there was never anything phony about it. It was the way he saw life. *"Wenn ich eine Predigt tue, so mache ich eine antithesin."* [26] Doberstein puts it this way:

> He never proclaims God's great Yes, God's acceptance of man in the gospel, without at the same time proclaiming his No, his rejection of all of man's presumption, work-righteousness and the imaginations of his reason. [27]

That was an expression of his insight that the sermon is part of the battle still going on between God and evil for the universe. And a battle always has two sides. The sermon is not just instruction, but conflict—of truth with error, God with Satan. There is the deepest kind of conflict within the reconciliation which God achieves through the gospel. It is a part of life that will not end this side of the grave. It makes Luther's sermons vibrant, powerful, in touch with life as the hearer lives it. He could preach that way because he had come through great conflict, lived with conflict in his own soul, but also knew the Victor whose presence and promise made it possible to survive in the midst of the conflict without being drained or overcome by it.

Luther in the pulpit

What was Luther like in the pulpit? His prayers before preaching speak volumes about that. Many pastors have the famous sacristy prayer which Lutheran tradition ascribes to him framed in their study or sacristy. Those who are just beginning their ministries could do worse than to hang it next to their desk or at the entry to the chancel:

O Lord God, dear Father in heaven, I am indeed unworthy of the office and ministry in which I am to make known thy glory and to nurture and to serve this congregation. But since thou hast appointed me to be a pastor and teacher, and the people are in need of the teaching and the instruction, O be thou my helper and let thy holy angels attend me. Then if thou art pleased to accomplish anything through me, to thy glory and not to mine or to the praise of men, grant me, out of thy pure grace and mercy, a right understanding of thy Word and that I may also diligently perform it.

O Lord Jesus Christ, Son of the living God, thou shepherd and bishop of our souls, send thy Holy Spirit that he may work with me, yea, that he may work in me to will and to do through thy divine strength according to thy good pleasure. Amen.[28]

In my seminary days prayer, rather than a set of stoles, was one of the standard ordination gifts. Another prayer that Luther often used before mounting the pulpit was, "Dear Lord God, I want to preach so that you are glorified. I want to speak of you, praise you, praise your name. Although I probably cannot make it turn out well, won't you make it turn out well?"[29] For him, preaching constituted the highest praise of God, even higher than prayer —an idea we would all do well to ponder.

Even as an old and experienced preacher, Luther was always fearful before he preached. If it were not for the constraint of obedience to the call of the God-ordained preaching office, he said, he would never walk up the steps of a pulpit. Never did he become blasé or self-confident about the preaching task. Never would he be able to understand anyone who said: "I really like to preach. That's my strong point, my cup of tea. That's what I enjoy most of all." He never lost his sense of the responsibility of the office and the danger of speaking for God.

> When one for the first time mounts the pulpit, no one would believe how very afraid one is! One sees so many heads down there! [Even now] when I am in the pulpit I look at no one but tell myself they are merely blocks of wood which stand there before me, and I speak the word of my God to them.[30]

This was not the fear of the young priest at the altar immobilized by the thought of a sinner holding the holy God in his hands, but rather the holy awe of being allowed to speak for the gracious God, to have God on his tongue by being faithful to the word, coupled with the profound desire to do it well, to the glory of God and to the benefit of the hearers. It was the fear of faith, the kind with which every explanation of the Commandments begins: "We should fear and love God so that we. . . ."

It is strange how little Luther's contemporaries said about his manner in the pulpit. It is said that he spoke slowly but with great vigor and that he often had a moving effect on the hearers. People liked to hear him, but his biographers and note-takers do not say what it was that appealed to them in his manner of preaching. James Mackinnon refers to his "torrential speech alive with prophetic fire," [31] but I have found no such descriptions from his contemporaries. We may confidently say that everything about his preaching was genuine. The message was everything. Histrionics, calculated gestures, anything done for effect would have been regarded as a human intrusion on the word of God. Although there was humor, there was never levity, or anything calculated to produce laughter. Yet the congregation frequently must have chuckled.

Legends about Luther's preaching manner abound, as you might expect. The latest one to come to my attention was in the form of a question: Is it true that the reason pulpits in Lutheran churches are on the right [when facing the front] rather than on the left, as in pre-Reformation churches, is that Luther's vigorous right-hand gestures often resulted in his skinning his knuckles against the wall?

I have found no contemporary descriptions of the quality, depth, and volume of his voice, except that his singing voice was a pleasant tenor. Luther said of Justus Jonas that the people didn't like him because he spit, sniffed, and cleared his throat too much. Either Luther had no idiosyncrasies, or his contemporaries were too kind to mention them. Surely his many opponents would not have hidden them if they had been obvious or distracting.

What the observers do agree on is that what he said was understood by all.

> He who teaches most simply, childishly, popularly . . . that's the best preacher. I like it to be easy and earthy. But now if it is debate you are looking for, come into my classroom! I'll give it to you plenty sharp, and you'll get your answer, however fancy your questions.[32]

On this score he did what he advised others to do:

> In the pulpit we are to lay bare the breasts and nourish the people with milk because every day a new church is raised up. . . . Therefore just preach the catechism faithfully and distribute the milk. Complicated thoughts and issues we should discuss in private with the eggheads [Kluglinge]. I don't think of Dr. Pomeranius, Jonas, or Philip in my sermon. They know more about it than I do. So I don't preach to them. I just preach to Hansie or Betsy [Elslein].[33]

On another occasion he added that if the presence of so many highly educated people scares you, just tell yourself "that you are the most educated of all when you speak from the pulpit." [34]

"The preacher must avoid laying emphasis on his own words in order to show off *[glänzen]*. . . . That is pure noise, serving one's own vanity. . . . To say much in a few words, not to blow up a little bit into a big form with many words, that is the art [of preaching]. [35]

Luther's words and illustrations were those of the common people: "God has chickens on earth who eat his grain and [then] lay their eggs elsewhere." [36] In reference to the need to straighten out the body of a deceased person in a casket he sometimes called death "old stretch-your-leg." [37] Those who expected food and money to increase because they had become Christians he called "knights of the belly." [38] On idea of merit, he said, "If a great good work would accomplish anything [toward salvation] asses and horses would also earn the kingdom of heaven." [39] Just going to church and hearing the word of God will not make one a Christian: "Dogs also occasionally stray into church and remain dogs as before." [40]

Pictures from nature were among his favorites: "You would hang your head if you would look at a bird . . . [singing] as its matins the *Te Deum Laudamus*." [41] Flowers are called wreaths worn by girls and doctors that show us how to trust God's goodness. He compared the Christian church to a beehive, with God as a queen bee who has neither stinger nor wrath. Because we are always so concerned about earthly things — food, dress, shelter — "we stick our snouts into the soup." [42]

Harold Grimm has culled many of these sayings from Luther's 1528-32 sermons, including: "He who cannot sing, always wants to sing." [43] "A believing Christian belongs to a rare race. He is like a black swan." [44] But not everyone was enthralled, or else Luther would not have said that the people sometimes "sleep and snore [during the sermon] until the rafters crack" [45] or "sleep and cough when we preach the article of justification but prick up their ears at [as soon as we tell] stories." [46] On the Seventh Commandment, he said, "Artisans and butchers should write ["Thou shalt not steal"] on the scales, the millers on their sacks, the bakers on their bread, the shoemakers on their lasts. . . . The poor people whom you cheat go out of the butcher shop crying . . . to heaven. . . . A market place should not be a den of thieves." [47] Just watch out, he said; someday those helpless cries will come back down around your head!

For Luther the simplicity of the Gospels was the standard he would apply to all preaching. Christ himself is the great example in the way he tailored everything to his audience. Because the hearers knew about sheep and shepherds, wolves, vineyards, fig trees, reeds, fields, and plowing, the Lord spoke about them. This was more than just a tactic for Luther. The incarnation itself is to shape preaching. Just as the Son of God humbled himself, became one of us, and lived the life we live, so preachers, though they speak from high above the people, should be one of them and speak as one of them. And because sermons are childlike, their very form is to show that the wonderful reality of God, to whom we are to bow in faith, is in fact very simple.

On this point Emanuel Hirsch observes, "To this day, this great inner simplicity has remained a mark by which to distinguish truly evangelical preaching. . . . We are not to give out a whole host of instructions [for living] but only to speak the truth which elicits faith." [48] "I must yet write a book against clever preachers," [49] said Luther in his later years. He was always amazed at how simply and in parables Christ dealt with the most profound things. I have not begun to read all his sermons, but one Luther scholar says that they became more and more simple toward the end of his life, concentrating ever more on the heart of the faith and expressed in ever more childlike ways. Chapter 3 cites some examples from his later sermons.

Was Luther also crude from the pulpit? Was he a spewer of filth, as the preecumenical anti-Luther literature of Catholicism charged? In all of my reading for these lectures I found only a few expressions that, even from our very different 20th-century perspective, could not be used in our churches. Much is made of his calling people "asses," but we must remember that the word *jackass [Esel]*, uncomplimentary as it is, did not have the double meaning of our word *ass*. To say that Jesus gave the Pharisees a whack on their tails is hardly the height of vulgarity. To use words like *stink* and *manure* about good works may offend some sensitive urban noses, but to Wittenbergers—for whom that commodity was a daily walking hazard (or to someone like me who not only worked summers on a farm but even liked cleaning out stables)—it is less offensive than poor grammar.

Occasionally Luther went far beyond what we would call good taste, but his own age did not make his use of language a point of criticism. In his last sermon in Wittenberg (1546), he spoke of people who let reason pervert the gospel: "I wish they had to eat their own dirt. . . . You cursed whore [reason], shut up! Are you trying to seduce me into committing fornication with the devil?" [50] He had no inner psychological need to shock his hearers. He knew why he was in the pulpit. It was not to entertain, show off, please his hearers, build his self-image, or to dazzle. It was to glorify Christ.

If your main impression of Luther's sermons has come from the *Martin Luther Christmas Book* of Roland Bainton, you will be surprised at how unstructured his actual sermons usually were. In the *Christmas Book* it is all concise, tightly packed, a flowing narrative — logical, but alive and exciting. We must remember that Bainton condensed dozens and dozens of Christmas sermons down to their best points and reassembled them for our age. You would probably look pretty good, too, if someone of Bainton's skill did that with your sermons over 30 years. I can see it now — *The Fred Meuser Seminary Chapel Book.* And the students and colleagues who had actually heard my sermons would say, "It sounds a bit familiar, but if his sermons were this good, how come we don't remember them that way?"

Johann Gerhard described Luther's preaching as "heroic disorder."[51] The main point of the text came first. From then on there was often a verse-by-verse exposition, but with the main point never far away. His preaching was always pastoral, and always consistent in the sense that they emphasized the overwhelming grace of God to sinful, unworthy, and helpless persons. Luther did have a plan for the sermon, his so-called *Konzept.* But Paul Althaus puts it just right when he says, "Luther's sermons were born in the pulpit."[52] They were conceived in the study and born in the pulpit. "The whole is not undisciplined, but it is unregulated, uncalculated, alive, like a free-flowing stream, while the later Lutheran *Schulpredigt* resembled a canal —symmetrical, careful, calculated, but hardly alive."[53]

Often Luther let himself be led to and fro by some particular scripture verse. For him, every word was an inexhaustible well. Repetition of similar thoughts was frequent. If, after having left the thought of one verse, he remembered something he wanted to say, he just went back to it. In many sermons he chased some rabbit or other across the landscape, and then had to come back to what he was talking about. In the good sense of the word, he just let himself go. Not that he was verbose — he scorned preachers who just spouted words.[54] But in him there was fullness of faith, insight, experience, love, and personal dynamic whose inherent extemporaneity could never be harnessed.

Sometimes Luther even forgot his *Konzept* or deliberately took a different line of thought. Once while preaching on Matthew, he forgot his whole *Konzept* while praying before the sermon. A *Table Talk* reference of Dec. 4, 1536, quotes him as saying, "It has often happened to me that my best *Konzept* has just gone to pieces [which is God's way of showing us] that He the Lord God alone means to be the preacher." [55] On another occasion he said,

> When I left the pulpit and thought over the sermon, I found that I had preached nothing or very little of what I had prepared. . . . We often preach quite differently from the way we plan because the Lord God gives us a different sermon. [56]

A letter by Luther to a discouraged young preacher reflects a good deal of his experience over the years:

> If Peter and Paul were here, they would scold you because you wish right off to be as accomplished as they. Crawling is something, even if one is unable to walk. Do your best. If you can't preach an hour, then preach a half hour or a quarter of an hour. Do not try to imitate other people. Center on the shortest and simplest points, which are the very heart of the matter and leave the rest to God. Look solely to His honor and not to applause. Pray that God will give you a mouth and to your audience ears. . . . You will most certainly find out three things: First you will have prepared your sermon as diligently as you know how, and it will slip through your fingers like water; secondly, you may abandon your outline and God will give you grace. You will preach your very best. The audience will be pleased—but you won't. And thirdly, when you have been unable in advance to pull anything together, you will preach acceptably both to your hearers and to yourself. So pray to God and leave all the rest to him. [57]

And after the sermon? How did he feel? Did he share the range of emotion that preachers today experience? I have already referred to his pointed warning against pride.

Only someone who was tempted to pride in his preaching could talk like that. As on many subjects, one can come up with apparent contradictions. On the one hand, he could say, "The Lord God is the real preacher," and on the other, "I have often preached [so poorly] that I have disgraced myself [and said to myself] Shame on you. What kind of a sermon was that." [58] He said that when one has preached, one must then above all other times ask God for forgiveness for not having done justice to the word.

But the opposite theme occurs often enough to be a fitting conclusion to this chapter:

A preacher must not pray the Lord's Prayer or ask for forgiveness of sins when he has finished preaching (not if he is a true preacher). Rather with Jeremiah he must say and boast, "Lord you know that what has come out of my mouth is right and pleasing to you." With St. Paul and all apostles say defiantly "Here God speaks." God Himself has said it. *Et iterum.* I was an apostle and prophet of Jesus Christ in this sermon. Here it is not necessary, not even good, to ask for forgiveness of sin, as if one had taught wrongly. For it is God's word and not mine which God neither can nor should forgive me, but [He should] confirm, praise and crown it and say, "You have taught rightly, for I have spoken through you and the word is mine." Whoever cannot speak like that about his sermon should leave preaching alone for he surely denies and blasphemes God. [59]

Luther's Gift
for Preaching

Samples of Luther's preaching
The hen and the chicks

The year was 1521. Luther sat alone at the Wartburg
Castle with a price on his head. He was fair game for any
bounty hunter and had no idea how long he might live.
His hearing before the emperor was over. His words, "Here
I stand — I can do no other" had taken him beyond the
point of return. The Roman church had made its move.
Luther's lectures, sermons, and writings were far too dis-
turbing even to be tolerated, much less approved. Priests,
bishops, theologians, and the pope himself had not only
turned their backs on him but had brought the full weight
of the church's power to bear on him. He was out of the
communion, beyond the pale, consigned to the wrath of
God. He had been spirited away to the Wartburg for safe-
keeping and had grown a full beard to hide his identity.

There he wrote a sermon on Matt. 23:34-39 to be included in his book of helps for those priests who were
eager to preach the Christ of the cross and the resurrection: [1]

> Woe to you scribes and Pharisees, hypocrites. . . . You
> blind guides . . . who strain a gnat and swallow a camel
> . . . full of extortion and rapacity . . white-washed tombs
> . . . full of hypocrisy and iniquity . . . sons of those who
> murdered the prophets . . . serpents, brood of vipers . . .
> upon you may come all the righteous blood shed on earth,
> from . . . Abel to . . . Zechariah . . . whom you mur-
> dered between the sanctuary and the altar . . . [You]
> kill the prophets and stone those who are sent to you.

What an opportunity this text provided to blow his opponents out of the water! If ever the big guns of denunciation
and wrath were to be rolled out, that was the time. And as
we know so well, Luther was a canoneer who could load,
aim, and blast away with the best of them.

But there were no broadsides. After a few comments
about God's efforts to reach Jerusalem, a more extensive
analysis of the present controversy about grace, faith, and
works, and some explanatory words about Abel, Zechariah,
and Barachiah (he pointed out that Scripture usually calls
him Jehoida), he built the sermon around the picture of
the hen and the chicks. Perhaps as he wrote he was watch-
ing a hen and her chicks in the castle courtyard below.

> The Lord sets up such a lovely picture and parable about
> faith and the believer, that I know of nothing lovelier in
> all of Scripture. . . . The Lord, in the most affectionate
> manner possible, demonstrates here to the Israelites his
> good will and kindness, saying that he would like to be
> their mother-hen, if [only] they had wanted to be the
> chicks. . . . When you look at the mother-hen and her
> chicks you see a picture of Christ and yourself better than
> any painter could paint.
>
> . . . our souls certainly are the chicks, and the devils and
> evil spirits are the hawks in the air, only we are not so
> clever as the chicks who take refuge under the mother-
> hen. . . . [Christ's] righteousness [is] to be [our] shelter and
> shield, even as the chick does not rely on its life and speed,

but seeks shelter under the mother-hen's body and wings.
. . . [So] under this righteousness [the chick] creeps,
snuggles, and crouches . . . trusts and believes . . . that
it will keep him protected. . . . Oh, we must remain in
Christ, on Christ, and under Christ and must not leave the
mother-hen. Otherwise everything is lost.

He pointed out how meticulously a mother-hen takes
care of her chicks:

It changes its natural voice turning it into a lamenting,
mourning one; it searches, scratches for food and lures the
chick to eat. When the mother-hen finds something, she
does not eat it, but leaves it for the chicks; she . . . calls
her chicks away from the hawk; she spreads out her wings
willingly and lets the chicks climb under her and all over
her, for she is truly fond of them. . . . Similarly, Christ
has taken unto himself a pitiful voice, has lamented for us.
. . . He scratches in the Scripture, lures us into it, and
permits us to eat; he spreads his wings with his righteousness, merit, and grace over us and takes us under himself
. . . warms us with his natural heat, i.e., with his Holy
Ghost . . . and . . . fights for us against the devil. . . .
His two wings are the two testaments of Holy Scripture
which spread over us his righteousness and take us under
him. Scripture teaches this and nothing else, namely, how
Christ is such a mother-hen. . . .

His body is he himself or the Christian church, his
warmth is his grace and the Holy Spirit. Behold, this is
the loveliest mother-hen . . . but what happens? We re-
fuse to be chicks. . . . Indeed . . [the ones who won't
cling only to her] become hawks and boars; they devour
and pursue the chicks with the mother-hen, tear apart
wings and body. . . . But what will be their reward?
Listen, terrible things will befall them. [God] has taken
his word from them and drawn his wings close to himself. . . .

We [Gentiles] . . . too, have persecuted the mother-hen.
. . . Therefore . . . the gospel and the faith have become silent. . . . God allows us to be torn asunder and
trampled to pieces. . . . so that there is no more knowledge
of the faith, no Christian life, no love, no fruit of the Spirit
[but only] . . . hypocrites, who presume to be Christians
with their vigils, masses, foundations, bells, churches, re-
citations of the Psalter or of the rosary . . . saints . . . holy
days . . . fasting, pilgrimmages and all the other foolish-
ness without number. O Lord God, completely torn asunder,
completely trampled to pieces, O Lord Christ, completely
desolate and forsaken are we miserable men in these last
days of wrath? Our shepherds are wolves; our watchmen
are traitors; our protectors are enemies; our fathers are
murderers; our teachers are seducers. Alas, alas and alas!
When? When? When will your harsh wrath cease?

Yet Christ also offers consolation by predicting that some
day he will be greeted with the shout, "Blessed is he who
comes in the name of the Lord!" These words are not yet
fulfilled but some day they will be. Luther ended, "God
grant that the time is near — as we hope! Amen."

This relatively short sermon is worth reading even now.
Without lengthy digressions, it breathes the spirit and the
fullness of the text. Full of the gospel and expressed with
simple language, it has one simple illustration at its heart.

The Wise Men

A different side of Luther can be seen in a sermon on
the Wise Men. [2] This is a very long sermon, in which
Luther goes into great detail in discussing every verse. We
will confine ourselves to his comments on the refusal of the
Wise Men to return to Herod. Here we have a warning
not to go back to the false doctrines that lead us away
from God. Human doctrines impel us to anticipate God.
We desire to seize the initiative, to take things into our

own hands. God is then supposed to come along later and give approval:

> Let me give you one example. . . . Those who seem to be most able, teach our youth and tell them that they should gladly pray and go to church, and live a chaste and pious life. But they do not tell . . . how they should go about it or where to find it, as if it were sufficient to have taught them to be pious. If [they] should marry or enter holy orders, they think it is sufficient . . . to do so by themselves, they do not consult God or even acknowledge his presence. But after the step has been taken, then God is expected to come and see what they have done and to regard the matter with favor and approval. Truly, young people are brought up in such a way that a girl is ashamed to ask God for a boy, or the boy for a girl. They think it foolish to make such a request known to God and prefer to stumble blindly into it themselves. That is why marriages are so rarely successful [this in 1522!]. Should we not rather teach a girl in all seriousness to come into God's presence confidently saying: Behold God, I have reached the age where I can marry, be thou my Father and let me be thy child, grant me a good man, and by thy grace help me to enter the estate of matrimony. Or if it be thy will, grant me the gift of chastity. Likewise a young man should pray for a girl and not initiate the matter by himself, but ask God to make a beginning and lay the first stone. Such are the true children of God who take no first step in any matter, however trivial, unless they have first addressed themselves to God about it. In this way Christ remains our king. . . . But the doctrines of men will not permit that; they stumble ahead blindly as if there were no God and all depended on them. . . . From this example you may well learn how seductive and contrary to God are the doctrines of men.

On change in the church

How does real change come in the church? Never by force, compulsion, or violence, said Luther, but rather by the persuasion of the word proclaimed in love. After his return from the Wartburg in 1522 he told the Wittenbergers:

> I see no signs of love among you [they had made radical changes while he was away]. . . . Here one can see that you do not have the Spirit, even though you have a deep knowledge of the Scriptures. . . .[3] Take myself as an example. I opposed indulgences and all the papists, but never with force. I simply taught, preached, and wrote God's Word; otherwise, I did nothing. And while I slept . . . or drank Wittenberg beer with my friends Philip and Amsdorf, the Word so greatly weakened the papacy that no priest or emperor ever inflicted such losses upon it. I did nothing; the Word did everything. . . . I could have brought great bloodshed upon Germany. . . . But what would it have been? Mere fool's play. I did nothing; I let the Word do its work. . . .[4] What do you suppose Satan thinks when one tries to get something done by force and violence?[5] He sits back there behind hell and thinks: "Oh, goody, what a fine game the poor fools are playing now! This is just what I like! I'll get plenty of booty out of it." Can't you just see the devil sitting there in his corner and laughing into the back of his hand, "Just let them go on! They're playing my little game—and I love it!"[6]

Such violence, added Luther, doesn't hurt Satan a bit, but when we spread the word, let it do its work, and love our neighbor and make their burdens our own, that distresses him greatly.

1 Peter 4:7-11

Spreading the word did not, however, always mean sweetness and light. On May 18, 1539, Exaudi Sunday, Luther preached on the Epistle that begins, "The end of all things is at hand; therefore keep sane and sober for your prayers" (1 Peter 4:7).[7]

Where one can find sermons which will stop the Germans from swilling I do not know. . . . The Italians call us gluttonous, drunken Germans and pigs.

Italians, Spaniards, and Turks were not like that, said Luther:

> [The Turks] make war and win; while we drunken sows sleep they keep awake. . . . When the time comes for us to defend ourselves and be prepared, we get drunk. This has become so widespread that there is no help for it; it has become a settled custom.

At first it was just the peasants, then the nobility. But then, said Luther, everyone, even the princes, was doing it. Ten-year-old milksops and students were ruining themselves. Those who should have put a stop to it did it themselves. Some young children, girls, and women were still sober, but one could find pigs among them, too.

> Germany is a land of hogs and a filthy people which debauches its body and its life. If you were going to paint it, you would have to paint a pig. . . .

> This gluttony and swilling is inundating us like an ocean . . . . We are the laughing-stock of all other countries. . . . We would not forbid [all drinking]; it is possible to tolerate a little elevation, when a man takes a drink or two too much after working hard and when he is feeling low. This must be called a frolic. But to sit day and night, pouring it in and pouring it out again, is piggish. This is not a human way of living, not to say Christian, but rather a pig's life. Eating and drinking are not forbidden [in Scripture] but rather all food is a matter of freedom, even a modest drink for one's pleasure. . . . if you are going to . . . be a born pig and guzzle beer and wine . . . you must know that you cannot be saved. For God will not admit such piggish drinkers into the kingdom of heaven. . . .

"Listen to the Word of God which says, 'Keep sane and sober,' " said Luther. Drunkenness is such a great sin and iniquity, "that it makes you guilty and excludes you from eternal life."

Such a sin is contrary to [our] baptism and hinders [our] faith and salvation. . . . If you wish to be a Christian, take care that you control yourself . . . "lest your hearts be weighed down with dissipation and drunkenness and cares of this life, and that day come upon you suddenly" . . . . If you are tired and downhearted, take a drink; but this does not mean being a pig and doing nothing but gorging and swilling.

Peter tells us why we should be sober. "Why? In order to be able to pray," because the devil prowls around "seeking someone to devour."

You must defend yourself with the Word and with prayer, not only for yourselves but the whole world. You are priests. . . . But when a man is drunk his reason is buried, his tongue and all his members are incapable of praying; he is a drunken pig and the devil has devoured him. . . .

God does not forbid you to drink, as do the Turks; he permits you to drink wine and beer; he does not make a law of it. But do not make a pig of yourself; remain a human being. . . . Keep your human self-control. . . .

"Sane" means that we should be alert and sensible. . . . "Sober" means that we should not overload the body, and it applies to excess in outward gestures, clothing, ornament, or whatever kind of pomp. . . . such as we have at baptisms and the churching of women. There is no moderation in these things. When there is a wedding or a dance you always have to go to excess. Christmas and Pentecost mean nothing but beer. Christians should not walk around so bedizened that one hardly knows whether one is looking at a man or a beast. We Christians ought to be examples.

"Above all" put on love. Drunkenness, Luther inferred throughout, makes love of neighbor impossible.

If you want to be saved, you must possess the red dress which is here described [which covers a multitude of sins]. You have put on the vestment [of Christ]. You are white as snow, pure from all sins. But you must wear this red dress and color now, and remember to love your neighbor. Moreover it should be a fervent love, not a pale-red love [a light pinkish love]. . . . It should be a strong color, a brown-red love, which is capable not only of doing good toward your neighbor but is also able to bear all malice from him. For this is the way sins are covered, even a multitude, a heap, a sea, a forest of sins. How? . . . It is another's love, namely, Christ's love, which has covered my sins. . . . He bore them in his body on the cross and erased them completely.

Since Christ did that, we are to bear with each other, forgive each other, and employ our gifts for one another.

After applying the love injunction to a variety of situations, Luther concluded, "When everything we do and say is in accord with God's Word, then the glory of Christ and God will be done to all eternity."

Although this sermon is strong, denunciatory, and even sarcastic in places, it is never legalistic. What he said about the Christian life in relation to alcoholic use was always an outgrowth of the gospel. His interest was never simply the negative objective of getting people to stop drinking. He did not resort to the so-called third use of the law. All of life, including the use or nonuse of alcohol, is to be an expression of the love of the neighbor as it flows out of the new life in Christ.

Whatever faults Luther's preaching may have had, people understood him, and he worked at being understood. Good communication is the subject of his treatise *On Translating*.[8] If you have never read it, or haven't for many years, pick it up when you're tired or need a break. It will give you many a chuckle and probably revive your spirits. I won't quote some of the harsher things he said about the people who criticized his translations but blatantly plagiarized them. Although it is a treatise and not a sermon, it shows how he communicated.

We do not have to inquire of the literal Latin, how we are to speak German . . . [but] we must inquire about this of the mother in the home, the children on the street, the common man in the marketplace . . . and do our translating accordingly. That way they will understand it and recognize that we are speaking German to them.

For example, Christ says: *Ex abundantia cordia os loquitur* . . . [our opponents translate] "Out of the abundance of the heart the mouth speaks." Tell me, is that speaking German? . . . What is "the abundance of the heart"? No German can say that; unless perhaps he was trying to say that someone was altogether too magnanimous or too courageous. . . . "Abundance of the heart" is not German, any more than "abundance of the house," "abundance of the stove," "abundance of the bench" . . . . But the mother in the home and the common man say this, "What fills the heart overflows the mouth." That is speaking good German.

And so also with the story of the precious ointment in Matthew 26 and Mark 14:

If I follow these literalistic asses I would have to translate it thus: "Why has this loss of ointment happened?" But what kind of German is that? What German says "Loss of ointment has happened"? . . . He [would] think(s) that the ointment is lost and must be looked for and found again. . . . A German would say *Ut quid*, etc. thus: "Why this waste?" Or, "Why this extravagance?" Indeed, "It's a shame about the ointment." That is good German. . . . That was what Judas meant. . . .

Again, when the angel greets Mary, he says "Hail Mary, full of grace, the Lord is with you!" . . . Tell me whether that is also good German! When does a German speak like that. "You are full of grace"? What German understands [that]? He would have to think of a keg "full of" beer or a purse "full of" money. Therefore I have translated it "Thou gracious one" so that a German can at least think his way through to what the angel meant. . . . Here, however, the papists are going wild about me, because I have corrupted the Angelic Salutation; though I have still not hit upon the best German rendering for it. Suppose I had taken the best German, and translated the salutation thus: "Hello there, Mary" [*Gott grüsse dich, liebe Maria*] for that is what the angel wanted to say, and what he would have said, if he had wanted to greet her in German. Suppose I had done that! I believe they would have hanged themselves out of tremendous fanaticism for the Virgin Mary, because I had thus destroyed the salutation. . . .

I shall say "gracious [*holdselige*] Mary," and "dear [*liebe*] Mary," and let them say "Mary full of grace [*volgnaden*]." Whoever knows German knows very well what a fine, expressive [*hertzlich*] word that word *liebe* is: the dear Mary, the dear God, the dear emperor . . . the dear child. I do not know whether the word *liebe* can be said in Latin or other languages with such fulness of sentiment that it pierces and rings through the heart [*das also dringe und kinge ynns hertz*], through all the senses as in our language.

How hard he struggled with the duty and determination to communicate well is reflected in what must have been a cry of weariness in the process of his translation of the Old Testament: "O God, what an arduous business to force the Hebrew writers to speak German! . . . It is like trying to compel a nightingale to eschew its most elegant melody and adopt, while detesting, the monstrous call of the cuckoo!" [9] Yet he was unusually skillful in every aspect of communication, not only because he knew the people, their needs, and their langauge. Our task, of course, is not to imitate his way of doing it, but to do for our age what he did for his.

Preaching the resurrection

Luther is surely better known as a preacher of Christ's death than of his resurrection. In the explanation of the Second Article in both the Small and the Large Catechisms Christ's death gets far more emphasis than the resurrection: ". . . he has saved and redeemed me, a lost and condemned person. He has freed me from sin, death, and the power of the devil — not with silver or gold, but with his holy and precious blood and his innocent suffering and death." The resurrection sneaks in almost by the side door, "that I may be his own . . . and serve him . . . just as he is risen from the dead. . . ."

Not so in his preaching. He loved to preach on the resurrection. It was a melody of his sermons even when it was not the theme. Luther would never have said what a friend of mine did some years ago, that he would rather preach ten Good Friday sermons than one on Easter. 1 Corinthians 15 was a special favorite of Luther's. More than once he preached a lengthy series of sermons on that classic resurrection chapter; in 1532-33 he preached 17 sermons in a row (from April to August) on that passage. During the Easter season he could hardly tear himself away from the resurrection theme. Perhaps the difference from our age is at least partly due to the fact that, unlike us, the 16th century had not learned to disguise death and hide from it as we have so expertly learned to do. Death was a visible and even an olfactory dimension of daily life that had to be faced.

Three days before Luther's death, in a dedicatory preface to a postil based on Jesus' words, "If anyone keeps my word he shall never see death," he said: "Unbelievable that is, but true — if one . . . believes and falls asleep in this word, then one dies and moves on [*fährt dahin*] before he is even aware of death and surely departs happy in the word [*selig im Wort*] which he has believed." [10] That is the way he talked and thought all his life. The trust in Christ that gives hope for this life and the life to come had its anchor and inspiration in the resurrection.

Death's defeat was no mere figure of speech to him. The resurrection is as much *pro nobis,* for us, as the crucifixion. Here, as in all the great events of Christ's life, Luther spoke of the "great exchange" which God offers us in Christ. Christ exchanges all of his beauty, peace, purity, and strength for our ugliness, turmoil, weakness, and death. He takes our death on himself and gives us his life. In his birth he takes our birth and exchanges his with us, "so that we become as pure and new in it as if it were our own." [11] In Christ's baptism he takes our sin and gives us his innocence; in his temptation our defeats in exchange for his steadfastness; in his passion our guilt in exchange for his forgiveness; and in his resurrection our death— our ultimate defeat — in exchange for his life. This wonderful exchange is a theme he could find in almost every text. What it means simply is that nothing in life or death can ever really harm the person who is hidden in Christ. His resurrected life begins in us now, will never cease, and will be fulfilled perfectly when he raises us up out of physical death.

This victory of Christ was always closely tied to the idea of a real, cosmic battle between God and Satan. Not even a shred of the idea that Easter proves our immortality appears in Luther, nothing of the perversion of Easter into a light-is-stronger-than-darkness, love-than-hate, life-than-death ideology so popular today. Nothing of the notion that Easter reveals some universal, natural truth about us and life and the world. His Easter hymn reflects his preaching:

> It was a strange and dreadful strife
> When life and death contended;
> The victory remained with life,
> The reign of death was ended. . . .

Our English translation of the next lines, "Death is swallowed up by death, Its sting is lost forever," [12] completely misses the earthy vigor of Luther's *"Wie ein Tod den andern frass, Ein Spott aus dem Tod ist worden. Hallelujah!"* As close as I can come to it is, "One death gobbled up (gulped down) the other, And made of it a laughing-stock. Hallelujah!" *Spott* is mockery—something we jeer at and make sport of. The color and dynamic slips away in the translation. But Luther's hymns and his preaching revel in the difference that Christ's breaking of the hold of death makes for the whole of life and the experience of death for Christians. He gave no explanation of how the victory was won and made no effort to prove it. He announced it, trusted it, reveled in it, and lived it.

Luther's love of conflict and drama made it impossible for him not to pick up on a resurrection idea popular in both the early and medieval church. It was, in fact, one of the oft-recurring themes of the medieval mystery plays — the duping or the tricking of Satan. God makes Satan blind to the fact that Jesus is the Son of God. He looks like just another poor, weak human being, vulnerable and easily taken. But God is like the fisherman who, in order to catch a fish, baits the hook with a worm. The fish thinks he has spotted a tasty morsel and swallows the worm. But inside the worm the sharp hook buries itself deep in the fish's throat, and he is caught, helpless. Christ's divinity is the hook hidden within his humanity. Satan spots the weak, suffering Jesus and gobbles him up. The hook then takes him captive. At times Luther gave the story a different twist: Christ is as indigestible and disagreeable as grass is to a dog. Christ sticks in Satan's throat, and he has to vomit him up as the whale did Jonah. In the very act of murderous gluttony, the devil throttles and chokes himself —and is taken captive by Christ. [13]

At the funeral of Duke John of Saxony on Aug. 18, 1532, Luther preached on 1 Thess. 4:13-14: "We would not have you ignorant, brethren, concerning those who are asleep. . . . For since we believe that Jesus died and rose again, even so, through Jesus, God will bring with him those who have fallen asleep." His sermon is a beautiful, personal, sensitive, pastoral, and biblical proclamation of his Easter faith and hope. [14]

In comparison with Christ's death ours is but a sleep. His was ". . . so bitter . . . grandiose . . . [and] potent that it has baptized all the other dead, so that now they are called not dead, but sleepers." Christ's death was the real death, ours only a sleep.

> No better comfort can be found than to contemplate this death and see how . . . it has devoured all other deaths. . . . Look not at this dead body [of the prince, but] you have something higher and better to contemplate, namely, the death and resurrection of Jesus Christ. . . . Even though it is hard, we must learn to look at the death of Christ, through which our death is destroyed. . . . The Holy Spirit . . . mingles this sour vinegar [of our death] with honey and sugar, that our faith may . . . see the dead, not lying in the grave and coffin, but in Christ. . . . Even though the carcass be foul and stinking [the funeral was in mid-August] it makes no difference; turn your eyes and nose and all five senses away and remember . . . [that it] will rise up imperishable. . . .
>
> We ought to thank God unceasingly for his grace in also including our beloved elector in the death of Christ and embracing him in his resurrection.

His real death he suffered at the Diet of Augsburg two years ago where he "openly confessed Christ's death and resurrection before the whole world and stuck to it, staking his land and people, indeed his own body and life upon it." Christ's death and the death John suffered at Augsburg were "real death." Physical death, when we pass away in bed, is only a little baby death [Kindersterben. The inference in Luther makes one think of children "playing dead"]. So it was for the prince. He did not labor, struggle, despair, break out in a cold sweat as some do. That is real death — the *fear* of death. But when one dies as he died, wrapped up in our Lord Christ's suffering, that is a baby death, only half a death. Our real death has already occurred when we died with Christ and were raised up with him into new life.

> It is my hope that we too shall die this way . . . if only we . . . wrap ourselves in the death of the Son of God and cover and veil ourselves with his resurrection. If we stand firmly upon this . . . [then] all our sins . . . will be as a tiny spark and our righteousness as a great ocean, and our death will be far less than a sleep and a dream.

> Hence, one must look upon a Christian death . . . not the way a cow stares at a new gate, and smell it in a different way, not as a cow sniffs grass, [but] by learning to speak and think of it as the Scriptures do. . . . [They are not] dead and buried people . . . [but] they are sleeping in Christ and God will bring them with Christ. . . . It is far more certain that Duke John of Saxony will come out of the grave and be far more splendid than the sun is now, than that he is lying here before our eyes.

The devil, of course, tries to snatch from our eyes the image of the man who died and rose again by asking me,

> . . . how good and how evil I am, and, what is more, he makes very masterful use of the Scriptures. . . . Then I make haste to seize hold of the article of the forgiveness of sins through Jesus Christ . . . and this is precisely what he does not want to let into my heart . . . [because] when I believe this with my whole heart, then I have the greatest treasure. . . . [Then I can say] devil, begone with both my righteousness and my sin. If I have committed some sin, go eat the dung; it's yours. I'm not worrying about it, for Jesus Christ died. . . . Go away and [come back]

some other time when I have been a bad boy. . . . This is not the time for arguing, but for comforting myself . . . that Jesus Christ died and rose for me.

God will carry me and all other Christians through death and hell. "Therefore, they should not be called dead people but sleeping . . . and such a deep sleep that one will not even dream; as without doubt our beloved lord and prince lies in a sweet sleep and has become one of the holy sleepers . . . not because he was a mild, merciful, kindly master, but because he confessed Christ's death and clung to it."

His death is a reminder of ours. "Therefore humble yourself and improve your life, that you, like him may be among those who suffer and die with Christ. . . . May God grant this to us. Amen."

Although it is a key point in Luther's theology that the cross and suffering are not removed from the lives of Christians, nevertheless, the new resurrection life of faith begins here and now. When preaching about Abraham he said, "Faith does not float on the heart like a goose on water, but it fashions a different mind and attitude and makes one an altogether new being." What is left of death is no different than if the devil gave you a "bitter little drink as we give people to put them to sleep so they feel nothing. But we will awaken again . . . when the trumpet sounds. The devil can't prevent it — we are already with Christ more than half-way through death so that he cannot even hang onto our poor old pouch or this [old] bag of worms." When the fear of death is gone, he said in his touching lectures on Abraham and Isaac, death is not death anymore. It is "nothing but a sport and empty little bugaboo of the human race, yes, an annoyance and a trial, as, for example, if a father sports with his son, takes an apple away from him, and meanwhile is thinking of leaving him the entire inheritance." [15] Such faith terrifies the demons, delights the angels, and comforts the godly.[16] The resurrected life in us is still a hidden life, as if we see the sun through the clouds, but we experience it, we do not just believe it. In another sermon he said, "for the person in whom selfishness and egotism have died in Christ, death is already past. [17]

One neat little turn I cannot resist including is from his lectures on Genesis 3, which show Luther having a bit of fun with a text. Commenting about the promise in Gen. 3:15 of the seed of the woman who would crush the head of the serpent, Luther says that God did not tell Satan which seed would do it. So from then on Satan would be afraid of all mothers, afraid every time a child was born. "He is thereby mocking Satan and making him afraid of all women." [18]

Luther's preaching was always filled with pictures. His awareness that he was hinting at that new life rather than describing it gave him the freedom to let his imagination run. In royal freedom and childlike faith he let the passage "unless you become as little children" shape his preaching. In one of the 1 Corinthians 15 sermons he said: "The whole world fears death above all and yearns for life above all else. This treasure, life, we will have without any limits and forever in him because God himself is life. If you would want, heaven's rain would be pure pieces of silver and nuggets of gold. The Elbe would flow with nothing but pearls and jewels. The world would be filled with all kinds of delights so that if you spoke to a tree it would bear only silver leaves and golden apples, the grass and flowers of the field would glisten like emeralds and all sorts of precious stones. In short: whatever gives you delight and joy will be there in abundance, because it is written, God himself will be all in all. But where God is, there everything good that one could wish for must be. People think, 'If I have all things, I have God.' But this makes a person a slave. The fact is, 'When I have God, I have all things.' This makes one free and makes the slave a child in God's fatherhouse. That is the *Herrlichkeit in Ewigkeit,* for which we pray in the Lord's Prayer." [19]

> God will be all in all. . . . everyone will have in God what we now have in things. . . . In God we will have so much that no food or drink or *Malvasier* [fine wine] will be so . . . nourishing as just one glance of God himself. That will make you stronger and more refreshed, healthier and happier, brighter and more beautiful than sun and moon, than all the clothes and golden robes worn by a king or caesar. They will be like mud in comparison with the beauty which one divine glance will suffuse over and in us. [20]

Yet with all his glowing language and contagious faith, Luther knew from his own experience how hard it was to believe in the resurrection when he stood at a coffin or saw a corpse carried out of the church. From his own heart he knew all the arguments and objections against the possibility of Christ's resurrection and ours. How hard it is, he often said, for this article to penetrate the heart. Human reason and wisdom are determined to get in the way of the resurrection. How can it be? is the question the devil raises to keep us from enjoying the blessing of the resurrection. That is why Luther so often called our insistence on comprehending spiritual realities "the great whore." It was not because he despised the mind and its marvelous powers, but only because so much of God's wisdom transcends our understanding. "If we are not content to rest on the word, then it is impossible for reason to believe anything. . . . So I tell my people: 'Beware of asking how or of trying to figure it out. You are in paradise if you close your ears to *Quare* ["why"] and just cling to the word.' " [21]

To insist on understanding in matters of faith is one more instance of relying on our own powers, our works — in this case our powers of understanding. Going it alone, without God, really means that we are left all alone in the battle with sin, self, life, and death. If here, at the resurrection, we rely on ourselves, then we shut the Victor out of our lives. That makes shipwreck of justification; it undercuts the article on which the church stands or falls just as surely as when one rejects the offer of forgiveness in Christ as a gift.[22]

Luther's own struggle for faith as well as his pastoral spirit were combined with his love of nature in a May 25, 1544, sermon, once again on 1 Corinthians 15. In the courtyard of the cloister that was his home for over 30 years stood a cherry tree, or more than one, that gave him great delight. He may well have been looking out of his window or sitting in the garden when this analogy was born.

Yes, you say, how can dead bodies come out of the grave, since they have rotted and returned to earth. How is that possible? Aha, you're a wise one all right![23] You think it's impossible because everybody rots and decomposes in the earth. . . . [But] Christ in his resurrection has gone before us and broken the path and [paved] the way, so that we follow him. Therefore we need not doubt this article.

Look at creation, he said, how:

". . . through God's . . . power life comes out of death. Go to the cherry tree, at Christmas . . . and you will not find a single green leaf on the whole tree or any . . . life. . . . But come back after Easter and the tree begins to come to life: the wood is full of sap and the shoots start to develop eyes and nodules. Closer to Pentecost the eyes become buds. When they open up out come little white blooms. When the blooms open you see a little stem. Out of the stem comes a kernel which is harder than the tree. [The] inside of the hard kernel is . . . somewhat softer, so that it can be used as food, somewhat like the marrow in the bone. Outside of and around the hard kernel grows the cherry—covered with a skin, like flesh and bone grow within our skin. The cherry grows so perfectly round *[so fen lustig rund]* that no lathe expert could do as good a job.

How does it happen that from the cherry tree's shoot which at Christmas was dry and dead as a broom-twig, a nodule begins to grow and out of the nodule a white flower, and out of the flower a stem and from the stem a kernel which inside has another kernel and outside produces a cherry? At first the stem is such a tiny little point in the little flower that one could hardly push the point of a needle through it. And yet a kernel grows in it and the kernel has marrow, flesh, blood, and skin. Isn't that a wonderful creation of God? No creature could make something like that, no person . . . however powerful, no doctor however educated or wise could make a single little cherry. And if we didn't see it every year we would never believe that out of a dry shoot such a beautiful desirable fruit could grow in such a wonderful way.

Where does the cherry tree come from? Doesn't it come out of the dry dead kernel? When the birds eat the cherries off the tree and the seeds stay on the stems they dry out, fall down under the tree, or are spread around elsewhere in the garden. We walk around on them without ever noticing. A year later a little tree shoots up out of the seed. Year after year it grows so that after ten or twenty years it is a very large tree and instead of one kernel from which it grew it produces many thousands of cherries.

Do you say at Easter—Ha! How can a cherry come forth from the nodule or a tree from the seed? You fool, haven't you ever seen it before? Wait till St. Margaret's day and I'll show you all the cherries which have grown out of the nodules. And then check whether after one year or two or five or ten a large tree hasn't appeared where now only a little seed lies.

So my dead little know-it-all, open your eyes and look at
the cherry tree. It will preach to you about the resurrection
of the dead and teach you how life comes out of death.[24]

Luther often preached with a natural childlikeness that
we, in our supposedly more sophisticated world, would
have a hard time doing. Yet even he was accused of speaking too much of commonplace things:

Yes, you say that the cherry tree business is common-place
and occurs every year. Therefore it can't be regarded as a
miracle because you see it with your own eyes, while you
do not see that the dead rise again. Thank you very much,
Mr. Know-it-all, that you push God's miracle out of sight
and talk so stupidly and without understanding about his
creation. Isn't it a sin and a shame that you so pass by
God's . . . work as if you were a clod or a stone without
any understanding? You have eyes, ears, reason and senses,
and yet aren't as smart as a cherry tree. Sure, your mouth
says 'I believe in God, the Father almighty, creator of heav-
en and earth.' But you do not believe it in your heart and
don't pay attention to what he has made. Even though the
cherry tree thing . . . happens every year, it does not happen without God's power, activity, and omnipotence, that
cherries grow out of a dry dead twig, and cherry trees from
tiny little seeds. At the beginning of creation God said:
. . . 'Let the earth bring forth . . . trees which bring forth
fruit after their kind and have their own seeds.' This word,
spoken by the creator, brings forth the cherries out of the
dry twigs and the cherry tree out of the little seeds. . . .
In this way God preaches to us every day about the resurrection of the dead.[25]

Luther was perfectly well aware that he had not proved
the resurrection of the dead. Nor was he equating processes
of nature with the resurrection. His point was only that
human perception often deceives us. Refusing to believe
the resurrection promise only because we have not seen it

happen is as foolish as denying in the spring that the tree can bear cherries in the fall.

Even Luther's speculations were invariably rooted in Scripture. He did not, as so many of us are inclined to do, simply project his so-called noble ideas onto God in preference to what the Scriptures say. Scripture is authoritative for the faith and teaching of the church. Luther once read the story of Abraham and Isaac on Mt. Moriah for family devotions. When he had finished, Katie said, "I do not believe it. God would not have treated his own son like that." But Katie," Luther answered, "he did." [26] That's the way he preached. The Scriptures are the written record of the revelation of God in Christ. They are the one ground of certainty. The promises of God found there are the anchor of faith.

This emphasis on Scripture kept Luther's curiosity about the resurrection life within carefully prescribed bounds. What will eternity be like? Everything will be different—everything earthly will end — we will be with the Lord—God will be all in all. God alone will be the Lord — all will be changed: husband, wife, child, house and estate, servant and maid, marriage, government, and offices in life. And yet (here is an insight into the whole of Luther's theology) people will still be male and female. We will still be who we are. We may not bear children, keep house, or feed our bellies, but we will be fully human beings. That is, creation will not be transcended or negated. Respect for creation and the guarding of the goodness of created life was a primary theme for both his theology and his preaching. Personal life will be fulfilled and completed, but never shucked off in favor of a kind of existence beyond creation. There was no romantic claptrap about becoming angels, no caviling at the continuation of personal existence in a new era. The created world will be redeemed, renewed, and transformed, but not transcended. Between death and the resurrection we will be asleep but not out of existence, somehow still in fellowship with God. [27] How? Let others try to comprehend and explain. Luther was content to give assurance and to rejoice.

Will we know our loved ones? As far as I know Luther never dealt with this question in his sermons on 1 Corinthians 15. But on the last evening of his life, just a few hours before his death, he was pressed by friends for an answer. Even then as he sat at the table with them they were still plying him with questions. He responded:

> What did Adam do? He had never seen Eve before; he lay there and slept. . . . When he awoke, he did not say 'Who are you? Where did you come from?' but 'This is flesh of my flesh and bone of my bone.' How did he know that this woman did not spring forth from a stone? It was because he was filled with the Holy Spirit and had a true perception of God. In his [God's] perception and image we will be renewed in the life to come, so that we and father and mother will recognize each other face to face better than Adam and Eve did. [28]

That analogy again shows how he thought in biblical terms in all things and saw all reality biblically. His answer was not that God would not be so mean as to deprive us of the joy of our loved ones. Instead his point was that clearness of perception is part of the life that Christ renews in us. If we live in the presence of God, then we live in the clarity of God, a clarity in which we also recognize those to whom our hearts belonged on earth. If here we know them better than others because we loved them, then we will really know them there, where our perceptions will be even more sensitive and where no one will have anything to hide. [29]

Luther could not bypass the passage about each one being rewarded by God according to one's works done in the body. An interpretation had to be found that did not explain away that passage but that also left salvation by grace alone intact. Luther's "solution" was that there will be ". . . no differences of office—no prince, lord, preacher, or subordinate," but there will be a difference

> . . . according to the way we have worked and lived . . . one will have higher insight than another, as one has done or suffered more in his calling. . . . Thus, there will be differences and honor according to one's *Amt*. And yet there will be equally one God and Lord in all and one joy and blessedness. According to one's person no one will have or be more than another—St. Peter no more than you or I. But nevertheless there must be differences according to one's life *["der Werke halben"]* for God did not do through St. Paul what he did through Isaiah, and vice versa. Therefore, everyone will bring along one's labors through which we will shine and praise God. [30]

I have picked out only a few examples to illustrate Luther's gift for preaching. They could be multiplied hundreds of times. You may be able to cite better examples than I. But I wanted in this Easter season to concentrate on some of those. Let me know about the better ones. Having gotten back into church history (what a joy) and back into Luther (it was almost a vacation), I have no intention of dropping him once the Hein Lectures are over.

If the only reading you do is directed toward next Sunday's sermon, leave Luther alone. But if you make time for the kind of reading that waters the roots of your faith, if you can be stimulated by people who saw life and faith from a perspective quite different from ours, if you want a touch of preaching that nails the conscience, warms the heart, and sometimes tickles the funny-bone, if you have time to live with a self-giving *Seelsorger* of God's grace, if you can use a dose of preaching that is always vital and never insipid—full of genuine humility, saving glory, and very tender love for Jesus—then you have time to read Luther's sermons.

Luther was able to proclaim the wonderful news of God's amazing grace with childlike simplicity. Nothing greater can be said about this preacher or of the gospel he preached. In earthen vessels taken from German soil the living water of the gospel was poured out on a thirsty Christendom 500 years ago. To this day it has not lost its refreshing power.

Notes

Chapter 1

[1] TR (Tischrede) 3, 3143.

[2] WA (Weimar edition) 51, 517. See Peter Meinhold, "Luther und die Predigt," in *Das Wort und die Wörter*, Festschrift für Gerhard Friedrich (Bolz und Schulz, 1973), p. 118.

[3] Cited in Bruno Jordan, "Die Auferstehung Christi von den Toten in Luthers Osterpredigten," *Luther: Mitteilungen der Luthergesellschaft* 1955:13.

[4] WA 47, 229. "The people are lacking, inasmuch as they fail to realize that the preaching office has to do with the Word of our Lord God. They think it is only the parson's word, as under the papacy. Therefore, they fear (as they say) that we want to become papist again, and wish merely to lord it over them. We ministers and preachers are also lacking, inasmuch as we ourselves do not regard our teaching as the very Word of God. For when the people humble themselves before us we very soon begin to play the tyrant. This is now the trouble, which has always been in the world, that the hearers are afraid of the tyranny of the preachers, and the preachers always seek to play god over their hearers (TR 6).

[5] Heiko A. Oberman, "The Preaching of the Word of God in

the Reformation," *Harvard Divinity Bulletin* 25 (October 1960): 16.

6 Emanuel Hirsch, "Luthers Predigtweise," *Luther: Mitteilungen der Luthergesellschaft* 1954:16.

7 Ibid.

8 WA 10, I, 2, 51; cited also in John W. Doberstein, "Introduction to Volume 51," *Luther's Works*, vol. 51, xxf.

9 *"Wen's trifft, den trifft's";* cited in Emanuel Hirsch, "Gesetz und Evangelium in Luthers Predigten," *Luther: Mitteilungen der Luthersgesellschaft* 1954:54.

10 *Luther's Works* (hereafter LW) 51, 390-391.

11 WA 6, 567; LW 36, 116.

12 Cited in Gerhard Heintze, *Luthers Predigt über Gesetz und Evangelium,* Forschungen zur Geschichte und Lehre des Protestantismus (Munich: 1958), p. 68.

13 Ibid. See also WA 10, III, 361.

14 Cited in Martin Doerne, "Luther und die Predigt," *Luther: Mitteilungen der Luthergesellschaft* 1939:39.

15 *The Works of Martin Luther,* Lenker edition, vol. 12, p. 54.

16 James MacKinnon thinks it was closer to 10,000.

17 August Wenzel, "Luther's Preaching on Romans," paper submitted to Garrett Theological Seminary, 1968, p. 7.

18 Hirsch, "Gesetz und Evangelium," p. 58.

19 After writing these lectures I came across the recently published *Martin Luther Easter Book* by Roland Bainton (Philadelphia: Fortress, 1983). Of its 83 pages, only 13 are on the resurrection. Luther's resurrection preaching is so rich that it deserves more extensive treatment. See Chapter 3 of this book for some excerpts that are not in Bainton's volume.

20 WA 3, 12.

21 In *Interpreting Luther's Legacy,* Essays in Honor of Edward C. Fendt (Minneapolis: Augsburg, 1969), pp. 2-13.

22 See Gerhard O. Forde, *Justification by Faith: A Matter of Death and Life* (Philadelphia: Fortress, 1982).

23 WA BR 11, 4139.

24 Heintze, p. 65.

25 WA 37, 394-395.

26 The 1522 sermon is on Rom. 13:11-14, WA I, 2, 1-2: "*Lare*

ist so man predigt, das unbekandt ist und die leutt wissend
oder verstendig machen. Vormanen ist, so man reytzt und
anhellt an dem, so yderman schon weiss."

[27] Ulrich Neubach, *Predigt des Evangeliums: Luther als Predigt iger, Pädagoge, und Rhetor* (Neukirchenverlag, 1956).

[28] WA 25, 263; Oberman, p. 9.

[29] Doberstein, lxx-lxxi.

[30] Vilmos Vajta, *Luther on Worship: An Interpretation* (Philadelphia: Fortress, 1958), p. 69 cites WA 30, II, 621 as one example from Luther: "God's Word must have no mean enemies but the mightiest ones. So as to prove its power in defeating them. Such are these four companions: the flesh, the world, death, and the devil. This is why Christ is named the Lord Sabaoth, i.e. a God of hosts or warfare, who is always at war and contends within us."

[31] Ibid.

[32] Doberstein, xx.

[33] WA 11, 415-416; LW 39, 314.

[34] Elector John, who must have heard about Luther's decision not to preach anymore, wrote an encouraging letter on Jan. 18, 1530, in which he said pointedly that "next week you will for the praise of God and in response to our gracious will again preach a sermon and not neglect to do so." Cited in Paul Glaue, "Der Predigtmüde Luther," *Luther: Mitteilungen der Luthergesellschaft* 1929:72.

[35] Glaue, p. 71.

[36] WA 16, 116-117.

[37] *Luthers Predigten,* Georg Buchwald, ed., vol. 1, no. 4, cited in Ròland H. Bainton, *Here I Stand* (New York: New American Library, 1950), p. 352. (Hereafter cited as LP-Buchwald.)

[38] Cited in Glaue, pp. 75-76.

[39] Ibid.

[40] Johann Matthesius, *Das Leben des theuren Mannes Gottes Martin Luther,* cited in Glaue, p. 70.

[41] Cited in Glaue, p. 74.

[42] Ibid.

[43] LW 51, 222-227 passim.

[44] LW 51, 197-208 passim.

45 WA 30, II, 340-341.
46 Glaue, p. 81.
47 Cited in Heintze, p. 282.

Chapter 2

1 Among the note-takers were Georg Rörer, Kaspar Cruciger, Johannes Aurifaber, Konrad Cordatus, Veit Dietrich, Anton Lauterbach, Andreas Poach, Johannes Schlaginhaufen, and Johanne Stoltz.
2 LP-Buchwald II, 442.
3 Cited in Meinhold, p. 122.
4 See Chap. 1, p. 26.
5 TR 2, 2580.
6 TR 4, 5171: *Praedicator ascendat, operiat os, et destinat."* James Mackinnon notes, "The saying is more expressive in German—*Steig flugs auf, tu's maul auf, hör bald auf." Luther and the Reformation* (New York: Russell and Russell, 1930), IV, 313, n. 45.
7 WA 53, 218.
8 Cited in Hirsch, "Predigtweise," p. 19.
9 WA 12, 37; LW 53, 14.
10 TR 2, 2287.
11 WA 18, 163.
12 TR 4, 4691; LW 54, 361.
13 Cited in Meinhold, p. 124.
14 WA 15, 41; LW 45, 364.
15 Cited in Meinhold; also LW 45, 365.
16 Ibid.
17 WA 32, 64-65.
18 LP-Buchwald I, 555. Cited in Bainton, p. 349.
19 WA 47, 454.
20 Cited in Meinhold, p. 113.
21 Elmer C. Kiessling, *The Early Sermons of Martin Luther and Their Relation to the Pre-Reformation Sermon* (Grand Rapids: Zondervan, 1935), p. 57.
22 Some examples: the missionary preaching of the peripatetic monks who converted most of Europe, the preaching of the 11th- and 12th-century monks who eventually established the

immense medieval monastic orders, the Crusade preachers, Bernard of Clairvaux' Jesus-preaching, the Waldensees, and many others. There was, says Martin Schmidt, an "unquenchable longing for preaching" among the people at the dawn of the 16th century. He claims that the Dominicans and Franciscans gave up the cruciform style of church architecture in favor of huge "hall churches" with the pulpit located on one of the middle pillars. This development, he says, spared the Reformation the need to develop its own architectural style. "Luthers Predigt und unsere Predigt heute," *Luther: Mitteilungen der Luthergesellschaft* 1970:63.

[23] Emanuel Hirsch explores the influences of Augustine and Tauler on this new preaching approach of Luther's. From Augustine he learned the "pure, formless exposition of Scripture," as against the thematic sermon; also, the rejection of all artistic devices, all "learned showing-off," and the need to relate the sermon to the needs of the hearers. From Tauler he learned that the sermon must be "centered," that is, must have only one main point and that this point must be important enough to "lead into the depths." No superficial messages have any place in the pulpit. Also from Tauler he learned that all sermons must have the same objective—to relate the individual hearer to the living God. All of Tauler's sermons, says Hirsch, teach just one essential truth, deep and rich enough to be looked at over and over from different perspectives. For the shaping of Luther's preaching this influence was even more important than Augustine's, in spite of the fact that in understanding of the gospel and in style he was much closer to Augustine. "Predigtweise," p. 8.

[24] Cited in Doerne, p. 40.

[25] WA 27, 402.

[26] Cited in Hirsch, p. 22—"When I preach a sermon, I make an antithesis."

[27] LW 51: xx.

[28] John W. Doberstein, *Ministers' Prayerbook: An Order of Prayers and Readings* (Philadelphia: Muhlenberg Press, 1959), p. 130.

[29] Cited in Hirsch, p. 20.

[30] TR 4, 4719.

31 Mackinnon, p. 317.

32 TR 4, 5047. Cited in H. G. Haile, *Luther: An Experiment in Biography* (New York: Doubleday, 1980), pp. 233-234.

33 TR 3, 3421.

34 TR 3, 1590.

35 Cited in Heintze, p. 13.

36 LP-Buchwald I, 79. All of the following Buchwald edition citations are from Harold J. Grimm, "The Human Element in Luther's Sermons," *Archiv für Reformationsgeschichte* 49 (1958): 50-60.

37 LP-Buchwald I, 171.

38 LP-Buchwald I, 251.

39 LP-Buchwald I, 222.

40 LP-Buchwald I, 257.

41 LP-Buchwald I, 572.

42 LP-Buchwald I, 561.

43 LP-Buchwald I, 115.

44 LP-Buchwald I, 59.

45 LP-Buchwald II, 182.

46 TR 2, 2408.

47 LP-Buchwald I, 79.

48 Hirsch, "Predigtweise," p. 147.

49 TR 4, 5047.

50 LW 51, 376. A few examples of his more vulgar expressions: To Romanists who had sworn "on the souls" that recipients of both bread and wine would be damned, "I'll poop on your soul and your word—and a big pile, too" (*Ich setze einen Dreck auf deine Seele und Wort, und setze einen grossen drauf*), from Georg Buchwald, "'Zur Kenntnis der Predigt Luthers," *Luther: Mitteilungen der Luthergesellschaft* 1923: 23. Luther described the corrupt church and the papacy thus: "Your whore stinks inside and outside, has syphilis, pestilence, epilepsy, and all kinds of plagues." LP-Buchwald II, 629. Those who are envious of others, he said, "look only at the evil in people. As one says in German, 'You have looked at me through my rear end.'" Ibid., 311.

51 Paul Althaus, "Luther auf der Kanzel," *Luther: Mitteilungen der Luthergesellschaft* 1921:17.

52 Althaus, p. 18.

[53] Ibid.

[54] "When Mörlin and Medler and Magister Jacob [perhaps Schenk] preach, it is as if you knocked the bung out of a full barrel. There it spouts because it is full inside. But this verbosity does not impress or edify, though it may please some. It is better to speak deliberately so that the hearer may grasp the subject matter." TR 5, 5199.

[55] Cited in Neubach, p. 170.

[56] TR 4, 4719.

[57] TR 2, 2606-2607. Cited in Bainton, p. 350.

[58] TR 4, 4719, and TR 5, 6110.

[59] WA 51, 517.

Chapter 3

[1] "The Gospel for St. Stephen's Day": Matt. 23:34-39. LW 52, 89-101 passim.

[2] "The Gospel for the Festival of the Epiphany": Matt. 2:1-12. LW 52, 159-286 passim.

[3] LW 51, 71, 74.

[4] LW 51, 77-78.

[5] *Mit Gewalt und Umsturtz.*

[6] Schmidt, p. 71.

[7] LW 51, 291-299 passim.

[8] *On Translating: An Open Letter.* LW 35, 189-192 passim.

[9] Cited in Mackinnon, pp. 277-278.

[10] Cited in Fritz Dosse, "Tod und Auferstehung in Luthers Predigt," *Luther: Mitteilungen der Luthergesellschaft* 1939: 60.

[11] LW 52, 15.

[12] *Lutheran Book of Worship* 134, stanza 2.

[13] WA 20, 334-335. See also Jordan, p. 60.

[14] LW 51, 232-243 passim.

[15] LW 4, 116.

[16] LW 4, 121.

[17] Cited by Dosse, p. 75.

[18] LW 1, 193.

[19] Paraphrased from a citation in Dosse, pp. 71-72.

[20] Ibid.

[21] WA 29, 329-330.

[22] Jordan, p. 17.

[23] *Ei, wie bleibst du doch immer ein Hans Pfriem.* "*Pfriem*" is a shoemaker's tool. The expression is about those who think they know a lot more than they do.

[24] Cited in Schmidt, pp. 72-73.

[25] Cited in Schmidt, pp. 73-74.

[26] TR 1, 1033.

[27] Once he said that although the sleep of death is much deeper than ordinary sleep, we shall yet be conscious enough to hear God and the angels talking to each other. Julius Kostlih, *The Theology of Luther in Its Historical Development and Inner Harmony* (Philadelphia: 1897) II:577.

[28] From C. Hessenmeister, *Dr. Martin Luthers Wirken, Tod, und Begräbnis* (Braunschweig: 1846), pp. 35-36.

[29] Dosse, p. 74.

[30] Dosse, p. 73.